Other titles in the same series:
Pastissima! Pasta the Italian Way
Antipasti! Appetizers the Italian Way
Zuppe Risotti Polenta! Italian Soup, Rice & Polenta Dishes
Verdure! Vegetables the Italian Way
Carne! Meat Dishes the Italian Way
Pesce! Fish & Seafood the Italian Way
Dolci e Frutta! Sweets & Desserts the Italian Way

© McRae Books Srl 1998

Conceived, edited and designed by McRae Books Srl, Florence, Italy

Text: Mariapaola Dèttore
Photography: Marco Lanza
Set Design: Sara Vignozzi

Design: Marco Nardi
Translation from the Italian: Darryl Price (Koiné)
Editing: Alison Leach, Lynn McRae, Anne McRae
Illustrations: Paola Holguín

The Publishers would like to thank Eugenio Taccini (Montelup Fiorentino), Flavia Srl (Montelupo Fiorentino), La Tuscia (Lastra a Signa), and Alessandro Frassinelli for their assistance during the production of this book

Color separations: Fotolito Toscana, Florence, Italy
Printed and bound in Italy by Artegrafica, Verona
ISBN 88-88166-16-5

CONTENTS

INTRODUCTION

The recipes in this book are all variations on a single, timeless theme — the combination of flour and water, usually with the addition of yeast, to make bread or bread-based foods, such as focacce or pizza. Bread is one of our oldest foods; its invention almost certainly dates back to over a million years ago, to the time when humans first learned to cook using fire. It is so simple and basic that it is prepared in almost exactly the same way today as it was then. Perhaps these ancestral links explain some of the satisfaction to be had from kneading and folding the dough, and from the delicious smell and taste of freshly baked homemade bread!

Italian cooking, with its roots in a rustic, peasant lifestyle, holds a particularly rich store of bread dishes. Many of these, such as pizza and focacce, have become famous the world over. The recipes here will take you back to the authentic versions of these well-loved classics. But I have also gathered together some surprises, particularly in the chapters on filled breads and fried dishes. Many of these regional, rustic specialities are little-known outside of Italy. I hope you will enjoy them.

CURED MEATS AND CHEESES

Cured meats and cheeses are used extensively as toppings for pizza and focacce and as fillings for filled and regional breads. The variety of cheeses and meats available in a good store or supermarket in Italy is astonishing. Fortunately, as Italian cooking becomes more and more popular abroad, the range of locally made or imported products outside Italy is steadily increasing.

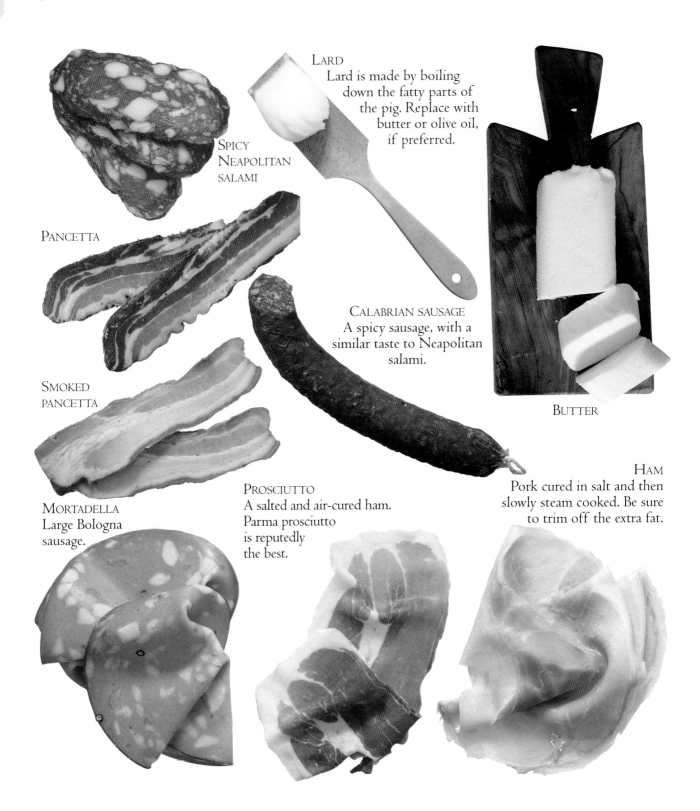

SPICY NEAPOLITAN SALAMI

LARD
Lard is made by boiling down the fatty parts of the pig. Replace with butter or olive oil, if preferred.

PANCETTA

CALABRIAN SAUSAGE
A spicy sausage, with a similar taste to Neapolitan salami.

BUTTER

SMOKED PANCETTA

HAM
Pork cured in salt and then slowly steam cooked. Be sure to trim off the extra fat.

PROSCIUTTO
A salted and air-cured ham. Parma prosciutto is reputedly the best.

MORTADELLA
Large Bologna sausage.

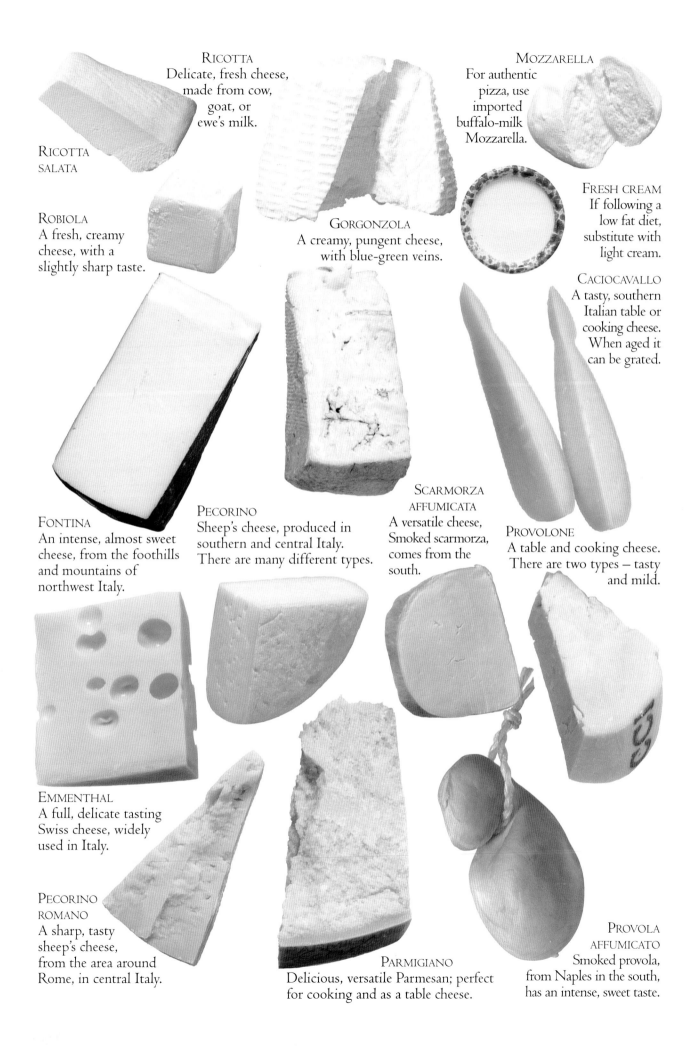

RICOTTA
Delicate, fresh cheese,
made from cow,
goat, or
ewe's milk.

RICOTTA
SALATA

MOZZARELLA
For authentic
pizza, use
imported
buffalo-milk
Mozzarella.

FRESH CREAM
If following a
low fat diet,
substitute with
light cream.

ROBIOLA
A fresh, creamy
cheese, with a
slightly sharp taste.

GORGONZOLA
A creamy, pungent cheese,
with blue-green veins.

CACIOCAVALLO
A tasty, southern
Italian table or
cooking cheese.
When aged it
can be grated.

FONTINA
An intense, almost sweet
cheese, from the foothills
and mountains of
northwest Italy.

PECORINO
Sheep's cheese, produced in
southern and central Italy.
There are many different types.

SCARMORZA
AFFUMICATA
A versatile cheese,
Smoked scarmorza,
comes from the
south.

PROVOLONE
A table and cooking cheese.
There are two types – tasty
and mild.

EMMENTHAL
A full, delicate tasting
Swiss cheese, widely
used in Italy.

PECORINO
ROMANO
A sharp, tasty
sheep's cheese,
from the area around
Rome, in central Italy.

PARMIGIANO
Delicious, versatile Parmesan; perfect
for cooking and as a table cheese.

PROVOLA
AFFUMICATO
Smoked provola,
from Naples in the south,
has an intense, sweet taste.

OTHER INGREDIENTS

The bland taste of the combination of flour, water, and yeast used to make bread and focacce, and pizza bases, goes perfectly with a truly wide range of accompaniments. These are a selection of many of the ingredients used in the recipes in this book.

CHILLI
PEPPERS

TOMATOES

GAETA OLIVES

BLACK OLIVES

BAKED OLIVES

"GREEK" OLIVES

GREEN OLIVES

EXTRA-VIRGIN
OLIVE OIL

TUNA

MUSSELS

ANCHOVY
FILLETS

ANCHOVIES
(salted)

FRESH
ANCHOVIES

BUTTON
MUSHROOMS
(Preserved in
olive oil)

CAPERS
(pickled)

CAPERS
(salted)

PORCINI
MUSHROOMS
(Preserved in olive oil)

GLOBE
ARTICHOKES
(Preserved in olive oil)

EGGPLANT
(AUBERGINE)

ESCAROLE

BASIL

CHIVES

GLOBE
ARTICHOKES

ASPARAGUS

FLAT-LEAF PARSLEY

LEEKS

ARUGULA
(ROCKET)

BELGIAN ENDIVES

PEAS

RED ONION

TARRAGON

GARLIC

OREGANO

SAGE

BELL PEPPER (CAPSICUM)

SWISS CHARD
(SILVER BEET)

SPINACH

YEASTS AND FLOURS

The popularity of making bread at home has greatly increased the number of different flours available. Any well-stocked supermarket or store has a wide range on its shelves. In Italy, fresh compressed yeast can be acquired by popping into the local bakery and asking for a piece; it is usually given free. Elsewhere it can be bought in small foil wrapped packets.

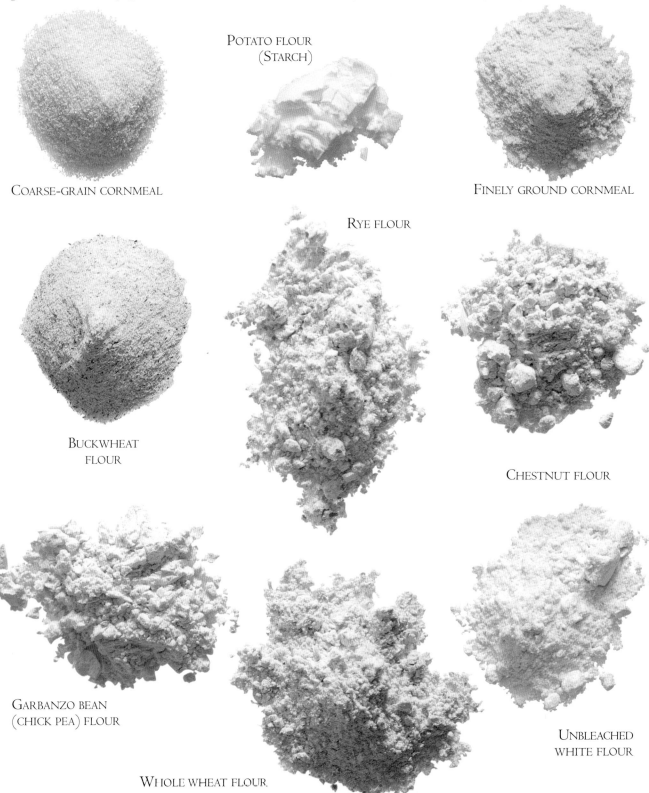

POTATO FLOUR (STARCH)

COARSE-GRAIN CORNMEAL

FINELY GROUND CORNMEAL

RYE FLOUR

BUCKWHEAT FLOUR

CHESTNUT FLOUR

GARBANZO BEAN (CHICK PEA) FLOUR

WHOLE WHEAT FLOUR

UNBLEACHED WHITE FLOUR

YEAST

I always use fresh compressed yeast because it produces the best bread and pizza. Be sure to check its expiry date when buying. If you can't get compressed yeast, use active dry yeast in its place. Remember that dry yeast is about twice as potent as the compressed variety. Active dry yeats is sold in packages weighing ¼ oz (7.5 g) each. The high-speed yeasts now available work very quickly, but the results are sometimes inferior.

COMPRESSED YEAST

ACTIVE DRY YEAST

SUGAR

SALT

The amount of salt given in the recipes reflects my personal taste. Experiment, and vary the amount used according to what you like.

WATER

The water for dissolving the yeast should be about 90–100°F (30–35°C). Use a thermometer at first; after a while you will know by just dipping your fingers in.

COARSE SEA SALT

FLOUR

Throughout this book I have recommended that you use unbleached white flour. This is because it it the type that most resembles the flour used for these recipes in Italy. However, you will find that most of the recipes can also be made successfully using all-purpose or plain white flour. The amount of water the flour absorbs will vary depending on the type of flour you are using. For this reason the quantities of water given in the recipes are approximate. Generally speaking, the amount of water needed is equivalent to around half the weight of the flour: given that it is easier to add more flour than it is to add more liquid, it may be advisable, especially when making the recipe the first couple of times, to keep a little flour to one side, ready to add if and when necessary. Remember that you will also need a couple of tablespoons extra to sprinkle the work surface, the surface of the dough and the baking sheet.

COOKING TIPS

For bread:

Cooking times will vary according to the type of oven (electricity or gas), and even among ovens of the same type. The times I have suggested are average cooking times and should be used as a guide. If you are using a fan (or convection) oven, the times will need to be reduced by a few minutes. Large and medium-sized loaves will require more time than rolls. Generally speaking, the bread will be cooked when the crust has turned golden brown. To check, once the suggested time has passed, remove the loaf from the oven, turn it over, and tap your knuckles against the bottom: if the bread is cooked it will make a clear, hollow sound. If it makes a dull, muffled sound then return it to the oven for another few minutes. This method is not very practical for smaller loaves and rolls, but after one or two attempts you will be able to instantly recognize when bread is ready by its aroma.

OVEN TEMPERATURE

Trial and error with your own oven is the only foolproof way of knowing the correct temperature for each dish. The temperatures given in the recipes are intended as guidelines. For example, 400°F/200°C/gas 6 for a gas oven will usually need to be about 450°F/230°C/gas 7 for an electric oven. Remember that unless otherwise stated, the oven must always be preheated so that the correct temperature has already been reached when it is time to put in the bread. When baking large loaves of bread, it is best to moisten the oven by placing a broiler pan or ovenproof bowl containing about 1½ cups of water on the oven floor 10 minutes before adding the bread.

For focacce:

The cooking times and oven temperatures given above for bread also apply for focacce. To check, tear off a little strip to see if the bottom is crisp and brown.

For pizzas and calzoni:

The cooking times and oven temperatures given above for bread also apply for pizzas and calzoni. You will know when pizzas and calzoni are ready by testing the dough around their edges. When cooked, it will be hard and crispy. You may also carefully tear off a little strip to check that the bottom is crisp and brown.

For filled breads and pies:

The cooking times and oven temperatures given above for bread also apply for the recipes in the filled breads and pies chapter.

PREPARING THE YEAST AND DOUGH

The dough for pizza, calzoni, bread, focacce and filled breads can be prepared in exactly the same way. The ingredients in the recipes may vary slightly, milk may be used instead of water, for example. Some recipes include additional ingredients, such as olive oil or lard. These should be added as indicated in the recipe while following the method given here.

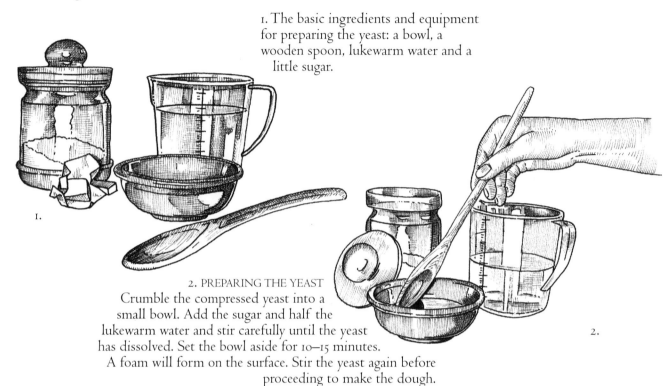

1. The basic ingredients and equipment for preparing the yeast: a bowl, a wooden spoon, lukewarm water and a little sugar.

2. PREPARING THE YEAST
Crumble the compressed yeast into a small bowl. Add the sugar and half the lukewarm water and stir carefully until the yeast has dissolved. Set the bowl aside for 10–15 minutes. A foam will form on the surface. Stir the yeast again before proceeding to make the dough.

1. The basic ingredients and equipment for making the dough: a large bowl, the flour, salt, yeast mixture, a wooden spoon and the remaining water.

2. MIXING THE DOUGH
Place the flour in a large bowl and sprinkle with the salt. Make a hollow in the flour and pour in the yeast mixture, the remaining water and any other ingredients listed in the recipe. Use a wooden spoon to stir the mixture. Stir well until the flour has almost all been absorbed.

HELPFUL HINT
Don't add all the flour at once. Reserve a little to add at the end, and mix it in only if necessary. Some flours absorb a lot of water, others require less.

3. PREPARING THE WORK SURFACE AND TRANSFERRING THE DOUGH

The dough will be a rough and shaggy ball in the bottom of the bowl. Sprinkle a work surface, preferably made of wood, with a little flour. Note that the flour used to prepare the work surface is not included in the quantities given for the doughs. You will need about ½ cup/50 g extra for this. Use a spatula (or your hands) to transfer the dough to the work surface. Curl your fingers around the dough and press it together to form a compact ball.

3.

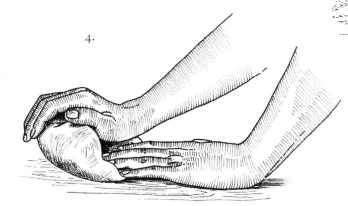

4.

HELPFUL HINT
Try not to mix in much extra flour as you knead. Too much flour absorbed during kneading will spoil the texture of the bread or pizza.

4.– 5. KNEADING THE DOUGH

Press the dough down to spread it a little. Take the far end of the dough, fold it a short distance toward you, then push it away again with the heel of your palm. Flexing your wrist, fold it toward you again, give it a quarter turn, then push it away. Repeat these motions, gently and with the lightest possible touch for about 7–8 minutes. When the dough is firm and no longer sticks to your hands or the work surface, lift it up and bang it down hard against the work surface a couple of times. This will develop the gluten. When ready, the dough should be smooth and elastic. It should show definite air bubbles beneath the surface and should spring back if you flatten it with your palm.

5.

6.

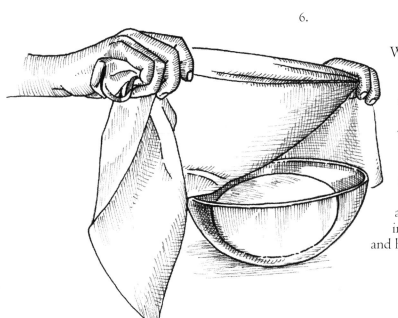

6. RISING

When the dough is fully kneaded, place it in a large clean bowl and cover with a cloth. Most of the breads in this book have two rising times, while the pizzas are left to rise just once. The dough should double in volume during rising. To test whether it has risen sufficiently, poke your finger gently into the dough and see if the impression remains; if it does, then the dough is ready.

The rising times given in each recipe are approximate; remember that yeast is a living ingredient and is affected by air temperature and humidity, among other things. Some days it will take longer to rise than others.

MAKING PIZZA AND CALZONI

The ingredients given here will make about 12 oz (350 g) of pizza dough. This is enough to make one round pizza, sufficient for one or two people.

■ INGREDIENTS

- ½ oz (15 g) fresh yeast or 1 package active dry yeast
- ⅔ cup (5 fl oz/150 ml) lukewarm water
- 2½–2¾ cups (8–10 oz/250–300 g) unbleached flour
- 1 teaspoon salt

Makes 1 pizza, about 12 in (30 cm) in diameter; Preparation: 30 minutes; Rising time: about 1 hour; Cooking: 15-20 minutes; Level of difficulty: Medium

Prepare the yeast and dough as explained on p. 12–13. § When the rising time has elapsed, knead the dough for 1 minute on a lightly floured work surface. § If you are making more than one pizza, divide the dough into the number of pizzas you wish to make. Roll each piece of dough into a ball and flatten a little with your hands. § Use your hands or a rolling pin to shape the pizza. To shape by hand, push the dough outward with the palms of your hands and fingertips, opening it out into a circular shape. Press the dough out, stretching it as you go, until it is the required thickness. Thickness depends on personal preference; some people like thick, doughy pizza crusts while others like them thin and crunchy. Experienced pizzamakers spread the dough by hand until it is about ½ in (12 mm) thick, then they pick it up and place it over their fists. By slowly moving their fists away from each other, they gently stretch the dough. They also bounce it the air and and twirl it on their fingertips. By all means, try one of these *virtuoso* performances when you feel confident enough. § To shape with a rolling pin, open the dough out into a circular shape of the desired thickness. § To finish, use your fingertips to make a rim around the edge of the pizza so that the topping won't drip out during cooking. § Transfer the dough to an oiled baking sheet. § The topping: there are two schools of thought about when the topping should be added. Some say it should go on straight away and the pizza go directly into the oven; others that the shaped pizza dough should sit for 10 minutes. I prefer to put the topping on straight away. You may choose whichever method you prefer.

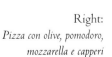

Right:
Pizza con olive, pomodoro, mozzarella e capperi

PLAIN PASTRY

Makes: pastry to line and cover a 10-in (25-cm) pan; Preparation: 10 minutes + 30 minutes to chill
Combine the flour in a large bowl with the salt. Make a hollow in the flour and fill with the egg, butter and water. Mix the ingredients with a fork, mashing the butter as you work. § After 2–3 minutes the dough will have absorbed almost all the flour. It should be quite crumbly. § Transfer to a lightly floured work surface and shape into a soft compact ball, kneading as little as possible. § Place in a springform pan or pie plate and flatten a little. Using the heels of your palms and your fingertips, spread the dough so that it covers the base of the pan evenly and three-quarters of the sides. Use a fork to shape the sides and bring to the same height. § Cover with plastic wrap and place in the refrigerator for at least 30 minutes. § This pastry can be a few hours ahead, or even the day before.

■ INGREDIENTS

- 2½ cups (8 oz/250 g) all-purpose (plain) flour
- 2 teaspoons salt
- 1 egg yolk
- ½ cup (4 oz/125 g) butter, at room temperature, thinly sliced
- 2 tablespoons water

RICOTTA PASTRY

Makes: pastry to line and cover a 10-in (25-cm) pan; Preparation: 10 minutes + 30 minutes to chill
Proceed as explained for plain pastry (above). Add the Ricotta when the flour and butter are almost mixed.

■ INGREDIENTS

- 2 cups (7 oz/200 g) all-purpose (plain) flour
- 2 level teaspoons salt
- ½ cup (4 oz/125 g) butter
- ⅓ cup (3½ oz/100 g) soft Ricotta cheese

PASTA MATTA
Special pastry

Makes: pastry to line and cover a 10-in (25-cm) pan; Preparation: 10 minutes + 30 minutes to chill
Combine the flour in a large bowl with the salt. Make a hollow in the flour and fill with the butter and water. Mix the ingredients with a fork, mashing the butter as you work. § When the ingredients are roughly mixed, transfer to a lightly floured work surface and knead until the dough is soft, smooth and elastic. § Flatten the dough with a rolling pin and shape it into a rectangle. Fold the shorter sides of the rectangle inward, one over the other. Roll the dough into another rectangle, working in the opposite direction to the folds. Fold the shorter sides of the rectangle inward again. Repeat the two steps once more. § Roll the dough into a rectangle or circle, depending on the pan or pie plate you are using. The dough should be about ¼ in (½ cm) thick. § Line the base and sides of the pan or pie plate, cover with plastic wrap and place in the refrigerator for at least 30 minutes.

■ INGREDIENTS

- 2½ cups (8 oz/250 g) all-purpose (plain) flour
- 2 teaspoons salt
- 4 tablespoons butter, at room temperature, thinly sliced
- ⅓ cup (3½ oz/100 g) cold water

Right:
Making Ricotta pastry

Pizza

*Invented in the backstreets of Naples, the
pizza has conquered the world. These are the classic
recipes of the truly Italian pizza.*

Pizza napoletana
Neapolitan pizza

Makes: 1 pizza, about 12 in (30 cm) in diameter; Preparation: 30 minutes; Rising time: about 1 hour; Cooking: 15-20 minutes; Level of difficulty: Medium

Prepare the dough as shown on pages 12–13. § When the rising time has elapsed, knead the dough for 1 minute on a lightly floured work surface. § Shape the pizza as explained on page 14 and transfer to an oiled baking sheet. § Spread the tomatoes evenly over the top, then add the Mozzarella, anchovies, and capers. Drizzle with 1 tablespoon of oil. § Bake in a preheated oven at 500°F/250°C/gas 8 for about 12 minutes. § Take the pizza out of the oven and sprinkle with the oregano. Return to the oven to finish cooking. § When cooked, drizzle with the remaining oil and serve hot.

Pizza marinara
Pizza with tomatoes and garlic

Marinara means sailor-style. The topping is made with tomatoes, olive oil, and garlic. No cheese is added because it doesn't go well with the most readily available food at sea — fish. This is one of the most traditional pizza toppings.

Makes: 1 pizza, about 12 in (30 cm) in diameter; Preparation: 30 minutes; Rising time: about 1 hour; Cooking: 15-20 minutes; Level of difficulty: Medium

Prepare the dough as shown on pages pages 12–13. § To peel the tomatoes, plunge them into a pot of boiling water for 30 seconds and then into cold. Slip off the skins, cut in half, and squeeze to remove some of the seeds. Place in a colander to drain for 10 minutes. § When the rising time has elapsed, knead the dough for 1 minute on a lightly floured work surface. § Shape the pizza as explained on page 14 and transfer to an oiled baking sheet. § Spread the tomatoes and garlic evenly over the top. Sprinkle with the oregano and salt and drizzle with 1 tablespoon of oil. § Bake in a preheated oven at 500°F/250°C/gas 8 for about 12 minutes. § Take the pizza out of the oven and sprinkle with the basil leaves. Return to the oven to finish cooking. § When cooked, drizzle with the remaining oil and serve hot.

■ INGREDIENTS

BASE
- 1 quantity pizza dough (see recipe p. 14)

TOPPING
- 8 oz (250 g) tomatoes, canned, drained and chopped
- 7 oz (200 g) Mozzarella cheese, thinly sliced
- 6 anchovy fillets,
- 1 tablespoon capers
- 3 tablespoons extra-virgin olive oil
- 1 heaped teaspoon oregano

Wine: a dry red (Rosso Vesuvio)

■ INGREDIENTS

BASE
- 1 quantity pizza dough (see recipe p. 14)

TOPPING
- 12 oz (350 g) ripe tomatoes
- 2 cloves garlic, thinly sliced
- 1 teaspoon oregano
- dash of salt
- 4 tablespoons extra-virgin olive oil
- 8 leaves fresh basil, torn

Wine: a dry rosé (Rosato del Salento)

Right:
Pizza napoletana

■ INGREDIENTS

BASE
• 1 quantity pizza dough
  (see recipe p. 14)

TOPPING
• 8 oz (250 g) tomatoes,
  canned, drained and
  chopped
• 7 oz (200 g) Mozzarella
  cheese, diced
• 4 tablespoons Pecorino
  romano cheese, freshly
  grated
• 4–6 anchovy fillets, crumbled
• salt and freshly ground
  black pepper
• 4 tablespoons extra-virgin
  olive oil
• 6 leaves fresh basil, torn

Wine: a dry white (Sylvaner)

■ INGREDIENTS

BASE
• 1 quantity pizza dough
  (see recipe p. 14)

TOPPING
• 8 oz (250 g) tomatoes,
  canned, drained and
  chopped
• 8 oz (250 g) Mozzarella
  cheese, thinly sliced
• dash of salt
• 1 tablespoon Parmesan
  cheese, freshly grated
  (optional)
• 3 tablespoons extra-virgin
  olive oil
• 9 leaves fresh basil, torn

*Wine: a dry rosé
(Lacryma Christi)*

Left: Pizza Margherita

PIZZA ALLA ROMANA
Roman-style pizza

Makes: 1 pizza, about 12 in (30 cm) in diameter; Preparation: 30 minutes; Rising time: about 1 hour; Cooking: 15-20 minutes; Level of difficulty: Medium

Prepare the dough as shown on pages pages 12–13. § When the rising time has elapsed, knead the dough for 1 minute on a lightly floured work surface. § Shape the pizza as explained on page 14 and transfer to an oiled baking sheet. § Spread the tomatoes evenly over the top and sprinkle with the Mozzarella, Pecorino romano, and anchovies. Season with salt and pepper and drizzle with 1 tablespoon of oil. § Bake in a preheated oven at 500°F/250°C/gas 8 for 15–20 minutes. § When cooked, sprinkle with the basil leaves, drizzle with the remaining oil, and serve hot.

PIZZA MARGHERITA
Pizza Margherita

According to legend, this pizza was created especially for Queen Margherita of Italy when she was staying in the royal palace of Capodimonte in Naples in 1889.

Makes: 1 pizza, about 12 in (30 cm) in diameter; Preparation: 30 minutes; Rising time: about 1 hour; Cooking: 15-20 minutes; Level of difficulty: Medium

Prepare the dough as shown on pages pages 12–13. § When the rising time has elapsed, knead the dough for 1 minute on a lightly floured work surface. § Shape the pizza as explained on page 14 and transfer to an oiled baking sheet. § Spread the tomatoes evenly over the top, cover with the Mozzarella and sprinkle with the salt and Parmesan, if using. Drizzle with 1 tablespoon of oil. § Bake in a preheated oven at 500°F/250°C/gas 8 for 15–20 minutes. § When cooked, sprinkle with the basil leaves, drizzle with the remaining oil, and serve hot.

VARIATION
– For a plain or White Margherita pizza, omit the tomatoes, and double the quantity of Parmesan. Add a generous grinding of black pepper just before serving.

Pizza alle acciughe
Pizza with anchovies

This delicious topping calls for fresh anchovies. If the thought of cleaning them seems daunting, ask your fish vendor to do it for you.

Makes: 1 pizza, about 12 in (30 cm) in diameter; Preparation: 30 minutes; Rising time: about 1 hour; Cooking: 12-15 minutes; Level of difficulty: Medium

Prepare the dough as shown on pages pages 12–13. § To clean the anchovies, remove the heads, slit the bodies open and discard the bones, then separate the two halves. If liked, leave them joined at the tail. Rinse well and pat dry with paper towels. § When the rising time has elapsed, knead the dough for 1 minute on a lightly floured work surface. § Shape the pizza as explained on page 14 and transfer to an oiled baking sheet. § Brush the dough with a little oil and arrange the anchovies on top. Sprinkle with the garlic, oregano, salt, and pepper. Drizzle with 1 tablespoon of oil. § Bake in a preheated oven at 500°F/250°C/gas 8 for 12–15 minutes. § When cooked, drizzle with the remaining oil, and serve hot.

Pizza al pomodoro
Tomato pizza

Makes: 1 pizza, about 12 in (30 cm) in diameter; Preparation: 20 minutes; Rising time: about 1 hour; Cooking: 10-15 minutes; Level of difficulty: Medium

Prepare the dough as shown on pages pages 12–13. § To peel the tomatoes, plunge them into a pot of boiling water for 30 seconds and then into cold. Slip off the skins, cut in half and squeeze to remove some of the seeds. Chop coarsely and set aside in a colander to drain for 10 minutes. § When the rising time has elapsed, knead the dough for 1 minute on a lightly floured work surface. § Shape the pizza as explained on page 14 and transfer to an oiled baking sheet. § Spread the tomatoes evenly over the top and sprinkle with the parsley, basil, salt, and pepper and drizzle with 1 tablespoon of oil. § Bake in a preheated oven at 500°F/250°C/gas 8 for 10–15 minutes. § When cooked, drizzle with the remaining oil, and serve hot.

VARIATION
– Sprinkle the pizza with 3 tablespoons of grated Parmesan or Pecorino cheese.

■ INGREDIENTS

BASE
• 1 quantity pizza dough (see recipe p. 14)

TOPPING
• 12 oz (350 g) fresh anchovies
• 3 tablespoons extra-virgin olive oil
• 2 cloves garlic, thinly sliced
• 1 teaspoon oregano
• salt and freshly ground black pepper

Wine: a dry white (Pomino)

■ INGREDIENTS

BASE
• 1 quantity pizza dough (see recipe p. 14)

TOPPING
• 12 oz (350 g) ripe tomatoes
• 2 teaspoons parsley, finely chopped
• 6 leaves fresh basil, torn
• 3 tablespoons extra-virgin olive oil
• salt and freshly ground black pepper

Wine: a young, dry red (Vino Novello)

Right:
Pizza alle acciughe

PIZZA AGLIO E OLIO
Pizza with garlic and oil

Makes: 1 pizza, about 12 in (30 cm) in diameter; Preparation: 30 minutes; Rising time: about 1 hour; Cooking: 10 minutes; Level of difficulty: Medium

Prepare the dough as shown on pages pages 12–13. § When the rising time has elapsed, knead the dough for 1 minute on a lightly floured work surface. § Shape the pizza as explained on page 14 and transfer to an oiled baking sheet. § Sprinkle with the garlic, oregano, salt, and pepper and drizzle with 1 tablespoon of oil. § Bake in a preheated oven at 500°F/250°C/gas 8 for 10 minutes. § When cooked, drizzle with the remaining oil, and serve hot.

INGREDIENTS

BASE
- 1 quantity pizza dough
  (see recipe p. 14)

TOPPING
- 2 tablespoons extra-virgin
  olive oil
- 4 oz (125 g) ham, sliced,
  and each slice torn in
  2–3 pieces
- 6 oz (180 g) Mozzarella
  cheese, diced
- freshly ground black
  pepper or ½ teaspoon
  crushed chillies (optional)

Wine: a dry red (Freisa d'Asti)

PIZZA AL PROSCIUTTO
Ham pizza

Makes: 1 pizza, about 12 in (30 cm) in diameter; Preparation: 30 minutes; Rising time: about 1 hour; Cooking: 15-20 minutes; Level of difficulty: Medium

Prepare the dough as shown on pages pages 12–13. § When the rising time has elapsed, knead the dough for 1 minute on a lightly floured work surface. § Shape the pizza as explained on page 14 and transfer to an oiled baking sheet. § Brush the dough with a little oil and arrange the ham on top. Sprinkle with the Mozzarella and the pepper (or chillies). Drizzle with 1 tablespoon of oil. § Bake in a preheated oven at 500°F/250°C/gas 8 for 15–20 minutes. § When cooked, drizzle with the remaining oil, and serve hot.

VARIATION
– Add 10 pitted black olives to the topping.

PIZZA ALLE OLIVE
Olive pizza

This pizza depends entirely on the quality of the olives. The small, dark, slightly bitter-tasting olives of Gaeta in southern Italy are perfect. If you can't get them, be sure to use high quality black olives packed in olive oil or brine imported from one of the Mediterranean countries rather than the tasteless pitted, canned varieties.

INGREDIENTS

BASE
- 1 quantity pizza dough
  (see recipe p. 14)

TOPPING
- 8 oz (250 g) tomatoes,
  canned, drained, and
  chopped
- 8–12 Gaeta olives
- 2–3 teaspoons capers
- 4–8 anchovy fillets,
  crumbled
- 3 tablespoons extra-virgin
  olive oil

Wine: a dry rosé (Salice Salentino)

Left: *Pizza al prosciutto*

Makes: 1 pizza, about 12 in (30 cm) in diameter; Preparation: 30 minutes; Rising time: about 1 hour; Cooking: 15-20 minutes; Level of difficulty: Medium

Prepare the dough as shown on pages pages 12–13. § When the rising time has elapsed, knead the dough for 1 minute on a lightly floured work surface. § Shape the pizza as explained on page 14 and transfer to an oiled baking sheet. § Spread with the tomatoes and garnish with the olives, capers, and anchovies. Drizzle with 1 tablespoon of oil. § Bake in a preheated oven at 500°F/250°C/gas 8 for 15–20 minutes. § When cooked, drizzle with the remaining oil, and serve hot.

Pizza capricciosa
Pizza with mixed topping

This is a modern recipe which has enjoyed great success. Capricciosa means "whimsical" and refers to the fact that there are no precise ingredients for the topping: choose whatever you like. These are the most commonly used ingredients.

Makes: 1 pizza, about 12 in (30 cm) in diameter; Preparation: 30 minutes; Rising time: about 1 hour; Cooking: 15-20 minutes; Level of difficulty: Medium

Prepare the dough as shown on pages pages 12–13. § When the rising time has elapsed, knead the dough for 1 minute on a lightly floured work surface. § Shape the pizza as explained on page 14 and transfer to an oiled baking sheet. § Spread the tomatoes evenly over the top, then add the ham, anchovies, Mozzarella, artichokes, mushrooms, olives and garlic. Sprinkle with oregano and drizzle with 1 tablespoon of oil. § Bake in a preheated oven at 500°F/250°C/gas 8 for 15–20 minutes. § When cooked, drizzle with the remaining oil, and serve hot.

Pizza al tonno
Tuna pizza

Makes: 1 pizza, about 12 in (30 cm) in diameter; Preparation: 35 minutes; Rising time: about 1 hour; Cooking: 15-20 minutes; Level of difficulty: Medium

Prepare the dough as shown on pages pages 12–13. § To peel the tomatoes, plunge them into a pot of boiling water for 30 seconds and then into cold. Slip off the skins, cut in half, and squeeze to remove some of the seeds. Set aside in a colander for 10 minutes to drain. § Transfer the tomatoes to a sauté pan with 1-2 tablespoons of oil, the garlic, and salt. Sauté for 4–5 minutes then set aside. § When the rising time has elapsed, knead the dough for 1 minute on a lightly floured work surface. § Shape the pizza as explained on page 14 and transfer to an oiled baking sheet. § Spread the tomato mixture evenly on top, then add the tuna, anchovies, olives, and capers. § Bake in a preheated oven at 500°F/250°C/gas 8 for 15–20 minutes. § When cooked, drizzle with the remaining oil, and serve hot.

VARIATION
– If you can't get fresh tomatoes, use 12 oz (350 g) of canned tomatoes, drained, and chopped.

■ INGREDIENTS

BASE
• 1 quantity pizza dough (see recipe p. 14)

TOPPING
• 7 oz (200 g) tomatoes, canned, drained and chopped
• 2 oz (60 g) ham, cut in strips
• 6 anchovy fillets, crumbled
• 4 oz (125 g) Mozzarella cheese, diced
• 2 oz (60 g) artichokes in oil, drained, and cut in half
• 2 oz (60 g) button mushrooms, cut in half
• 2 oz (60 g) green olives, pitted, and cut in thin rings
• 2 cloves garlic, sliced
• 1 teaspoon oregano
• 3 tablespoons extra-virgin olive oil

■ INGREDIENTS

BASE
• 1 quantity pizza dough (see recipe p. 14)

TOPPING
• 14 oz (450 g) fresh tomatoes
• 4 tablespoons extra-virgin olive oil
• 1 clove garlic, sliced
• dash of salt
• 7 oz (200 g) tuna packed in oil, drained and in chunks
• 8 anchovy fillets, crumbled
• 3 oz (90 g) black olives
• 1 tablespoon capers

Wine: a young, dry white (Trebbiano di Romagna)

Right: *Pizza capricciosa*

■ INGREDIENTS

BASE
- 1 quantity pizza dough
  (see recipe p. 14)

TOPPING
- 1 tablespoon lard
- 5 oz (150 g) fresh
  Pecorino cheese, sliced
- freshly ground black or
  white pepper
- 6 leaves fresh basil, torn

Wine: a dry white (Colli Albani)

PIZZA BIANCA
Classic plain pizza

Makes: 1 pizza, about 12 in (30 cm) in diameter; Preparation: 30 minutes; Rising time: about 1 hour; Cooking: 10-15 minutes; Level of difficulty: Medium

Prepare the dough as shown on pages pages 12–13. § When the rising time has elapsed, knead the dough for 1 minute on a lightly floured work surface. § Shape the pizza as explained on page 14 and transfer to an oiled baking sheet. § Spread with the lard, arrange the Pecorino on top and sprinkle with pepper. § Bake in a preheated oven at 500°F/250°C/gas 8 for 10–15 minutes. § When cooked, sprinkle with the basil and serve hot.

Pizza ai funghi

Mushroom pizza

Makes: 1 pizza, about 12 in (30 cm) in diameter; Preparation: 30 minutes; Rising time: about 1 hour; Cooking: 15-20 minutes; Level of difficulty: Medium

Prepare the dough as shown on pages pages 12–13. § Clean the mushrooms and rinse carefully under cold running water. Pat dry and slice thinly. § Sauté the mushrooms in 1 tablespoon of oil over very high heat for 2–3 minutes. Drain off any excess liquid and stir in the parsley and garlic. Set aside. § When the rising time has elapsed, knead the dough for 1 minute on a lightly floured work surface. § Shape the pizza as explained on page 14 and transfer to an oiled baking sheet. § Spread the mushrooms over the top and sprinkle with salt and pepper. Drizzle with the remaining oil and bake in a preheated oven at 500°F/250°C/ gas 8 for 10–20 minutes. § Serve hot.

Pizza quattro stagioni

Four-seasons pizza

Makes: 1 pizza, about 12 in (30 cm) in diameter; Preparation: 40 minutes + 1 hour to soak mussels; Rising time: about 1 hour; Cooking: 15-20 minutes; Level of difficulty: Medium

Prepare the dough as shown on pages pages 12–13. § Soak the mussels in a large bowl of water for at least 1 hour to purge them of sand. Pull off their beards, scrub, and rinse well in cold water. § Rinse the mushrooms, slice, and sauté in 1 tablespoon of oil over medium heat for 3–4 minutes. Season with salt and set aside. § Place the mussels in a large skillet (frying pan) over high heat. Stir frequently until the shells are open. Discard the shells of all but 4 mussels. Strain the liquid produced and set aside with the mussels in a bowl. § When the rising time has elapsed, knead the dough for 1 minute on a lightly floured work surface. § Shape the pizza as explained on page 14 and transfer to an oiled baking sheet. § Spread the tomatoes on top and sprinkle with salt. § Now, imagine the pizza divided into 4 equal parts: garnish one quarter with mushrooms, one with artichokes, one with olives and anchovies, and one with garlic. § Bake in a preheated oven at 500°F/250°C/gas 8 for 15–20 minutes. § When cooked, arrange the mussels on the quarter with tomato and garlic. Drizzle with the remaining oil and serve.

■ INGREDIENTS

BASE

- 1 quantity pizza dough (see recipe p. 14)

TOPPING

- 8 oz (250 g) porcini mushrooms, or white mushrooms plus ¾ oz (25 g) dried porcini
- 3 tablespoons extra-virgin olive oil
- 1 tablespoon parsley, finely chopped
- 1 clove garlic, finely chopped
- salt and freshly ground black pepper

Wine: a dry red (Grignolino)

■ INGREDIENTS

BASE

- 1 quantity pizza dough (see recipe p. 14)

TOPPING

- 5 oz (150 g) white mushrooms
- 3 tablespoons extra-virgin olive oil
- dash of salt
- 12 oz (350 g) mussels, in shell
- 7 oz (200 g) tomatoes, canned, drained, and chopped
- 3 oz (90 g) artichokes in oil, drained and halved
- 3 oz (90 g) black olives, pitted
- 2–3 anchovy fillets, crumbled
- 1 clove garlic, thinly sliced

Wine: a dry red (Chianti)

Right: *Pizza ai funghi*

Pizza ai quattro formaggi
Four-cheese pizza

*Vary the cheeses according to what you like (and what you have in the refrigerator).
Aim for a balance between texture and intensity of taste.*

*Makes: 1 pizza, about 12 in (30 cm) in diameter; Preparation: 30 minutes; Rising time: about 1 hour;
Cooking: 15-20 minutes; Level of difficulty: Medium*

Prepare the dough as shown on pages pages 12–13. § When the rising time has elapsed, knead the dough for 1 minute on a lightly floured work surface. § Shape the pizza as explained on page 14 and transfer to an oiled baking sheet. § Spread the surface with the cheeses and, if liked, sprinkle with crushed chillies. Drizzle with the oil. § Bake in a preheated oven at 500°F/250°C/gas 8 for 15–20 minutes. § Serve hot.

Pizza Sardenaira

Italian Riviera-style pizza

*This recipe comes from Liguria, on the Italian Riviera. A similar recipe exists
across the border in France, on the Côte d'Azur, where it is called the* Pissaladière.
Debate rages about the nationality of this pizza.

*Makes: 1 pizza, about 12 in (30 cm) in diameter; Preparation: 40 minutes; Rising time: about 1 hour;
Cooking: 20-25 minutes; Level of difficulty: Medium*

Prepare the dough as shown on pages pages 12–13, adding the oil to the flour mixture. § Sauté the onions in oil for 15 minutes, stirring frequently, until they are soft and lightly browned. Season with salt and pepper and set aside to cool. § When the rising time has elapsed, knead the dough for 1 minute on a lightly floured work surface. § Shape the pizza as explained on page 14 and transfer to an oiled baking sheet. § Spread the onions over the pizza and sprinkle with the olives, anchovies, garlic, and oregano, if using. § Bake in a preheated oven at 500°F/250°C/gas 8 for 20–25 minutes. Serve hot.

■ INGREDIENTS

BASE
- 1 quantity pizza dough (see recipe p. 14)

TOPPING
- 4 oz (125 g) Mozzarella cheese, diced
- 3 tablespoons Parmesan cheese, freshly grated
- 4 oz (125 g) Gorgonzola cheese, diced
- 3 oz (90 g) Emmental cheese, thinly sliced
- ½ teaspoon crushed chillies (optional)
- 1 tablespoon extra-virgin olive oil

■ INGREDIENTS

BASE
- 1 quantity pizza dough (see recipe p. 14)
- 2 tablespoons extra-virgin olive oil

TOPPING
- 10 oz (300 g) onions, thinly sliced
- 2 tablespoons extra-virgin olive oil
- salt and freshly ground black pepper
- 3 oz (90 g) black olives
- 12 anchovy fillets, crumbled
- 3 cloves garlic, finely chopped (optional)
- 1 teaspoon oregano (optional)

Wine: a dry white (Vermentino)

VARIATIONS
– Before adding the onions, spread the dough with 3–4 tablespoons of drained and chopped canned tomatoes.
– Add 1–2 tablespoons of capers to the topping.

Right: *Pizza Sardenaira*

Pizza siciliana
Sicilian-style pizza

Traditional Sicilian pizza has a thicker, softer base than pizza from northern Italy.
For this pizza, stretch the dough to a diameter of not more than 11 in (28 cm).

Makes: 1 pizza, about 11 in (28 cm) in diameter; Preparation: 30 minutes; Rising time: about 1½ hours; Cooking: about 30 minutes; Level of difficulty: Medium

Prepare the dough as shown on pages pages 12–13. § When the rising time has elapsed, knead the dough for 1 minute on a lightly floured work surface. § Shape the pizza as explained on page 14 and transfer to an oiled baking sheet. § Spread the tomatoes evenly over the pizza, and sprinkle with the basil, olives, and onion, followed by the Pecorino and oregano. Finish with the anchovies and drizzle with 1 tablespoon of oil. § Bake in a preheated oven at 500°F/250°C/gas 8 for about 30 minutes. § When cooked, drizzle with the remaining oil, and serve hot.

> VARIATION
> – Add 4 oz (125 g) diced Mozzarella cheese to the topping.

■ INGREDIENTS

BASE
- 1 quantity pizza dough (see recipe p. 14)

TOPPING
- 12 oz (350 g) tomatoes, canned, drained, and chopped
- 6 leaves fresh basil, torn
- 3 oz (90 g) black olives
- 1 small onion, thinly sliced
- 2 oz (60 g) Pecorino cheese, freshly grated
- 1 teaspoon oregano
- 4–6 anchovy fillets, crumbled
- 3 tablespoons extra-virgin olive oil

Wine: a dry rosé (Etna Rosato)

Pizza ai due formaggi
Two-cheese pizza

Makes: 1 pizza, about 12 in (30 cm) in diameter; Preparation: 30 minutes; Rising time: about 1 hour; Cooking: 10-15 minutes; Level of difficulty: Medium

Prepare the dough as shown on pages pages 12–13. § Combine the Ricotta, Gorgonzola, chives, garlic, cream, and oil in a bowl and mix thoroughly. § When the rising time has elapsed, knead the dough for 1 minute on a lightly floured work surface. § Shape the pizza as explained on page 14 and transfer to an oiled baking sheet. § Spread the topping evenly over the pizza and bake in a preheated oven at 500°F/250°C/gas 8 for 10–15 minutes. § Serve hot.

■ INGREDIENTS

BASE
- 1 quantity pizza dough (see recipe p. 14)

TOPPING
- ⅔ cup (5 oz/150 g) fresh Ricotta cheese
- 6 oz (180 g) Gorgonzola cheese, diced
- 2 tablespoons chives, finely chopped
- 1 small clove garlic, finely chopped
- 1–2 tablespoons fresh cream
- 1 tablespoon extra-virgin olive oil

Wine: a dry red (Pignoletto)

Left: Pizza siciliana

Pizza alle melanzane
Eggplant pizza

Makes: 1 pizza, about 12 in (30 cm) in diameter; Preparation: 40 minutes; Rising time: about 1 hour; Cooking: 15-20 minutes; Level of difficulty: Medium

Prepare the dough as shown on pages pages 12–13. § Cut the eggplant into slices ½ in (1 cm) thick and brush lightly with oil. § Grill for 3–4 minutes in a hot grill pan, turning them over only once. Sprinkle with salt, garlic, and parsley. Set aside. § When the rising time has elapsed, knead the dough for 1 minute on a lightly floured work surface. § Shape the pizza as explained on page 14 and transfer to an oiled baking sheet. § Spread the tomatoes evenly over the pizza and sprinkle with the Mozzarella. Drizzle with 1 tablespoon of oil. § Bake in a preheated oven at 500°F/250°C/gas 8 for 10–15 minutes. § Take the pizza out of the oven and cover with the slices of eggplant. Return to the oven for 5 minutes more. § When cooked, sprinkle with the basil, drizzle with the remaining oil, and serve hot.

■ INGREDIENTS

BASE
- 1 quantity pizza dough (see recipe p. 14)

TOPPING
- 10 oz (300 g) eggplant (aubergine)
- 3 tablespoons extra-virgin olive oil
- dash of salt
- 2 cloves garlic, finely chopped
- 1 tablespoon parsley, finely chopped
- 7 oz (200 g) tomatoes, canned, drained and chopped
- 5 oz (150 g) Mozzarella cheese, diced
- 6 leaves fresh basil, torn

Wine: a dry red (Chianti dei Colli Senesi)

Pizza ai peperoni
Pizza with bell peppers

Makes: 1 pizza, about 12 in (30 cm) in diameter; Preparation: 40 minutes; Rising time: about 1 hour; Cooking: 15-20 minutes; Level of difficulty: Medium

Prepare the dough as shown on pages pages 12–13. § Sauté the onion in 2 tablespoons of oil for 3 minutes over medium heat. Add the bell peppers and, after 1–2 minutes, the tomatoes and capers. Season with salt and cook, stirring continuously, for 5–7 minutes. § Add the basil leaves and turn off the heat. § When the rising time has elapsed, knead the dough for 1 minute on a lightly floured work surface. § Shape the pizza as explained on page 14 and transfer to an oiled baking sheet. § Spread the bell pepper mixture evenly over the pizza, sprinkle with the cheese, and drizzle with the remaining oil. § Bake in a preheated oven at 500°F/250°C/gas 8 for 15–20 minutes. § Serve hot.

■ INGREDIENTS

BASE
- 1 quantity pizza dough (see recipe p. 14)

TOPPING
- 1 small onion, sliced
- 3 tablespoons extra-virgin olive oil
- 12 oz (350 g) bell peppers (capsicums), cut in strips
- 7 cup (200 g) tomatoes, canned, chopped, not drained
- 1 tablespoon capers
- dash of salt
- 6 leaves fresh basil, torn
- 3 tablespoons Pecorino cheese, freshly grated

Wine: a dry sparkling red (Lambrusco)

Right: *Pizza ai peperoni*

■ INGREDIENTS

BASE
• 1 quantity pizza dough
  (see recipe p. 14)

TOPPING
• 4 globe artichokes
• juice of 1 lemon
• 4 tablespoons extra-virgin
  olive oil
• salt and freshly ground
  black pepper
• 4 oz (125 g) Fontina
  cheese, very thinly sliced

*Wine: a dry white
(Vernaccia di San Gimignano)*

Pizza ai carciofi
Artichoke pizza

Makes: 1 pizza, about 12 in (30 cm) in diameter; Preparation: 30 minutes; Rising time: about 1 hour; Cooking: 15-20 minutes; Level of difficulty: Medium

Prepare the dough as shown on pages pages 12–13. § Clean the artichokes by removing the stalks and tough outer leaves. Trim off and discard the tops. Cut in half and remove the fuzzy inner choke with a sharp knife. Place in a bowl of cold water with the lemon juice for 10 minutes. § Drain the artichokes, pat dry with paper towels, and slice thinly. § Transfer to a sauté pan with 1 tablespoon of oil and cook over medium heat for 3 minutes, stirring frequently. Season with salt. § When the rising time has elapsed, knead the dough for 1 minute on a lightly floured work surface. § Shape the pizza as explained on page 14 and transfer to an oiled baking sheet. § Brush the pizza with ½ tablespoon of oil and spread with the slices of artichoke. Season with salt and pepper and arrange the Fontina slices on top. Drizzle with 1 tablespoon of oil. § Bake in a preheated oven at 500°F/250°C/gas 8 for 15–20 minutes. § When cooked, drizzle with the remaining oil, and serve hot.

■ INGREDIENTS

BASE
• 1 quantity pizza dough
  (see recipe p. 14)

TOPPING
• 2 tablespoons butter
• 14 oz (450 g) leeks, sliced
• 3 oz (90 g) pancetta, diced
• salt and freshly ground
  black pepper
• 1 egg
• 1½ tablespoons fresh cream
• 4 tablespoons Parmesan
  cheese, freshly grated
• 2 oz (60 g) Gruyère
  cheese, very thinly sliced

Left: Pizza ai carciofi

Pizza ai porri
Leek pizza

Makes: 1 pizza, about 12 in (30 cm) in diameter; Preparation: 45 minutes; Rising time: about 1 hour; Cooking: 15-20 minutes; Level of difficulty: Medium

Prepare the dough as shown on pages pages 12–13. § Melt the butter in a sauté pan and add the leeks and pancetta. Sauté over medium-low heat for 10 minutes, stirring frequently. Season with salt and pepper and set aside to cool. § When the rising time has elapsed, knead the dough for 1 minute on a lightly floured work surface. § Shape the pizza as explained on page 14 and transfer to an oiled baking sheet. § Beat the egg with the cream in a bowl. Add the leek and pancetta mixture and the two cheeses. Mix well. § Spread the mixture evenly over the pizza and bake in a preheated oven at 450°F/230°C/gas 7 for 15–20 minutes. § Serve hot.

PIZZA ALLA RUCOLA IN BIANCO
Pizza with arugula and Mozzarella cheese

This is a modern classic. It has become extremely popular in pizzerias throughout Italy.

Makes: 1 pizza, about 12 in (30 cm) in diameter; Preparation: 30 minutes; Rising time: about 1 hour; Cooking: 12-16 minutes; Level of difficulty: Medium

Prepare the dough as shown on pages 12–13. § When the rising time has elapsed, knead the dough for 1 minute on a lightly floured work surface. § Shape the pizza as explained on page 14 and transfer to an oiled baking sheet. § Brush the surface with 1 tablespoon of oil and sprinkle with a little salt. § Bake in a preheated oven at 450°F/230°C/gas 7 for 6–8 minutes. § Take the pizza out of the oven and sprinkle with the Mozzarella. Return to the oven and cook for 6–8 minutes more. § When cooked, garnish with the prosciutto and arugula, drizzle with the remaining oil, and serve hot.

VARIATIONS
– Replace the prosciutto with the same amount of ham.
– Break the prosciutto, or ham, into pieces before garnishing the pizza.

■ INGREDIENTS

BASE
- 1 quantity pizza dough (see recipe p. 14)

TOPPING
- 2 tablespoons extra-virgin olive oil
- dash of salt
- 5 oz (150 g) Mozzarella cheese, sliced or diced
- 3 oz (90 g) prosciutto, thinly sliced
- ½ oz (15 g) arugula (rocket), washed, dried, and coarsely chopped

Wine: a dry white (Bianco di Pitigliano)

PIZZA ALLA RUCOLA IN ROSSO
Pizza with arugula, tomato, and Mozzarella cheese

Makes: 1 pizza, about 12 in (30 cm) in diameter; Preparation: 30 minutes; Rising time: about 1 hour; Cooking: 15-20 minutes; Level of difficulty: Medium

Prepare the dough as shown on pages 12–13. § When the rising time has elapsed, knead the dough for 1 minute on a lightly floured work surface. § Shape the pizza as explained on page 14 and transfer to an oiled baking sheet. § Spread the tomatoes evenly over the pizza and bake in a preheated oven at 500°F/250°C/gas 8 for about 10 minutes. § Remove the pizza from the oven, cover with the Mozzarella and drizzle with 1 tablespoon of oil. Return to the oven and cook for 6–8 minutes more. § When cooked, garnish with the arugula and a generous grinding of black pepper, if liked. Drizzle with the remaining oil and serve hot.

■ INGREDIENTS

BASE
- 1 quantity pizza dough (see recipe p. 14)

TOPPING
- 7 oz (200 g) tomatoes, canned, drained, and chopped
- 5 oz (150 g) Mozzarella cheese, sliced
- 2 tablespoons extra-virgin olive oil
- ½ oz (15 g) arugula (rocket), washed, dried, and coarsely chopped
- freshly ground black pepper (optional)

Wine: a young, dry red (Chianti)

Right: *Pizza alla rucola in bianco*

Pizza affumicata
Pizza with cheese and smoked pancetta

Makes: 1 pizza, about 12 in (30 cm) in diameter; Preparation: 30 minutes; Rising time: about 1 hour; Cooking: 15 minutes; Level of difficulty: Medium

Prepare the dough as shown on pages 12–13. § Cook the smoked pancetta for 2–3 minutes in a skillet (frying pan) over low heat, without adding any fat. Drain and cut into strips the width of a finger. § When the rising time has elapsed, knead the dough for 1 minute on a lightly floured work surface. § Shape the pizza as explained on page 14 and transfer to an oiled baking sheet. § Spread the pizza with the Robiola (or Crescenza), and sprinkle with the pancetta, followed by the cubes of Provolone. § Bake in a preheated oven at 500°F/250°C/gas 8 for 15 minutes and serve.

> VARIATION
> – For extra flavor, sprinkle the cooked pizza with 1 oz (30 g) of chopped smoked herring fillet.

■ INGREDIENTS

BASE
- 1 quantity pizza dough (see recipe p. 14)

TOPPING
- 4 oz (125 g) smoked pancetta, or bacon, sliced
- ½ cup (4 oz /125 g) Robiola, Crescenza, or similar soft, fresh cheese
- 5 oz (150 g) smoked Provolone cheese, diced

Wine: a dry red (Cirò)

Pizza alle cozze
Mussel pizza

Makes: 1 pizza, about 12 in (30 cm) in diameter; Preparation: 40 minutes; Rising time: about 1 hour; Cooking: 10-12 minutes; Level of difficulty: Medium

Prepare the dough as shown on pages 12–13. § Soak the mussels in a large bowl of water for 1 hour. Pull off their beards, scrub, and rinse in abundant cold water. § Place the mussels in a large skillet (frying pan) over high heat. Stir frequently. They will open after a couple of minutes. Discard the shells of all but 4 or 5 mussels. Strain the liquid the mussels have produced and set aside with the mussels in a bowl. § When the rising time has elapsed, knead the dough for 1 minute on a lightly floured work surface. § Shape the pizza as explained on page 14 and transfer to an oiled baking sheet. § Drizzle with 1 tablespoon of oil and bake in a preheated oven at 500°F/250°C/gas 8 for 8–10 minutes. § Drain the mussels. § Take the pizza out of the oven and arrange the mussels and remaining shells on top. Sprinkle with the parsley, garlic, oregano, salt, and pepper, and drizzle with the remaining oil. § Bake for 1–2 minutes more. § Serve hot.

> VARIATION
> – Mix 7 oz (200 g) of chopped tomatoes with the garlic, and drizzle all the oil over the base before baking.

■ INGREDIENTS

BASE
- 1 quantity pizza dough (see recipe p. 14)

TOPPING
- 2 lb (1 kg) mussels, in shell
- 3 tablespoons extra-virgin olive oil
- 1 tablespoon parsley, finely chopped
- 2 cloves garlic, finely chopped
- 1 teaspoon oregano
- salt and freshly ground black pepper

Wine: a dry white (Cinque Terre)

Right: Pizze rapidissime

■ INGREDIENTS

- 4 thick slices bread
- 4 tablespoons extra-virgin olive oil
- 8 oz (250 g) tomatoes, chopped
- 7 oz (200 g) Mozzarella cheese, sliced
- 4–8 anchovy fillets
- 1 tablespoon capers
- 1 teaspoon oregano

Wine: a dry red
(Merlot del Trentino)

PIZZE RAPIDISSIME

Quick pizzas

These "pizzas" are delicious and quick to prepare. Vary the toppings according to taste.

Makes: 4 "pizzas"; Preparation: 10 minutes; Cooking: 8–10 minutes; Level of difficulty: Simple

Brush both sides of the slices of bread with half the oil. § Spread the tomatoes on top, followed by the Mozzarella, anchovies, capers, and oregano. § Drizzle with the remaining oil and place on a baking sheet. § Bake in a preheated oven at 450°F/230°C/gas 7 for 8–10 minutes, or until the Mozzarella melts and turns pale gold. The bread should be crisp and lightly browned.

Calzoni

To make calzoni, *just* fold the pizza dough over the filling in a half-moon shape and bake in a hot oven.

Calzone alla napoletana
Neapolitan calzone

Makes: 4 calzoni; Preparation: 35 minutes; Rising time: about 1 hour; Cooking: 20-25 minutes; Level of difficulty: Medium

Prepare the dough as shown on pages 12–13. § Mix the Ricotta, Pecorino (or Parmesan), and eggs in a bowl. Add the Mozzarella, salami, and salt. Mix well and set aside. § When the rising time has elapsed, knead the dough for 1 minute on a lightly floured work surface, then divide into 4 equal portions. § Stretch the dough into circular shapes, about 9 in (23 cm) in diameter, as explained on page 14. § Spread the filling on one half of each calzone, leaving a ¾-in (2-cm) border around the edge for sealing. Fold the other half of the dough over the top, pressing down firmly on the edges to seal. § Arrange the calzoni on two lightly oiled baking sheets. Mix the tomatoes with 3 tablespoons of oil and the salt, and spread over the calzoni. § Bake in a preheated oven at 450°F/230°C/gas 7 for 20–25 minutes. The calzoni should be puffed and golden brown. § Serve hot.

■ INGREDIENTS

BASE
- 3 quantities pizza dough (see recipe p. 14)

FILLING
- 1 cup (8 oz/250 g) fresh Ricotta cheese
- 4 tablespoons Pecorino romano, or Parmesan cheese, freshly grated
- 2 eggs
- 8 oz (250 g) Mozzarella cheese, diced
- 4 oz (125 g) Neapolitan salami, diced
- dash of salt
- 4 tablespoons extra-virgin olive oil
- 3 oz (90 g) tomatoes, canned, drained and chopped

Wine: a dry red (Ischia)

Calzone alla pugliese con prosciutto
Apulian-style calzone with ham

Makes: 4 calzoni; Preparation: 35 minutes; Rising time: about 1 hour; Cooking: 20-25 minutes; Level of difficulty: Medium

Prepare the dough as shown on pages 12–13. § When the rising time has elapsed, knead the dough for 1 minute on a lightly floured work surface, then divide into 4 equal portions. § Stretch the dough into circular shapes, about 9 in (23 cm) in diameter, as explained on page 14. § Spread half of each calzone with the Ricotta, then sprinkle with the Mozzarella and ham, leaving a ¾-in (2-cm) border around the edge for sealing. Fold the other half of the dough over the top, pressing down firmly on the edges to seal. § Arrange the calzoni on two lightly oiled baking sheets. Mix the tomatoes with 2 tablespoons of oil and the salt, and spread over the calzoni. § Bake in a preheated oven at 450°F/230°C/gas 7 for 20–25 minutes. The calzoni should be puffed and golden brown. § Serve hot.

■ INGREDIENTS

BASE
- 3 quantities pizza dough (see recipe p. 14)

FILLING
- 8 oz (250 g) soft Ricotta cheese
- 8 oz (250 g) Mozzarella cheese, diced
- 8 oz (250 g) ham, thinly sliced
- 3 tablespoons extra-virgin olive oil
- 3 oz (90 g) canned tomatoes, drained and chopped
- dash of salt

Wine: a dry white (Orvieto Classico)

Right: Calzone alla napoletana

Calzone alle melanzane
Eggplant calzone

Makes: 4 calzoni; Preparation: 40 minutes; Rising time: about 1 hour; Cooking: 20-25 minutes; Level of difficulty: Medium

Prepare the dough as shown on pages 12–13. § Fry the eggplant in the oil in a large, heavy-bottomed pan over medium-high heat, stirring frequently. After 8–10 minutes, add the marjoram, garlic, salt, and, if necessary, a little more oil. Cook for 2–3 minutes more, until the eggplant is lightly browned. § Add the tomatoes, parsley, basil, and Pecorino. Stir for 1 minute then remove from heat. § When the rising time has elapsed, knead the dough for 1 minute on a lightly floured work surface, then divide into 4 equal portions. § Stretch the dough into circular shapes, about 9 in (23 cm) in diameter, as explained on page 14. § Spread the filling on one half of each calzone, leaving a ¾-in (2-cm) border around the edge for sealing. Fold the other half of the dough over the top, pressing down firmly on the edges to seal. § Brush the calzoni with the remaining oil and arrange them on two lightly oiled baking sheets. § Bake in a preheated oven at 450°F/230°C/gas 7 for 20–25 minutes. § Serve hot.

> VARIATIONS
> – Replace the marjoram with 1 teaspoon of oregano.
> – Omit the Pecorino and use the same quantity of Mozzarella cheese combined with 1 tablespoon of freshly grated Parmesan.

■ INGREDIENTS

BASE
- 3 quantities pizza dough (see recipe p. 14)

FILLING
- 1 lb (500 g) eggplant (aubergine), diced
- ½ cup (4 fl oz/125 ml) extra-virgin olive oil
- 3 tablespoons fresh marjoram, finely chopped
- 1 clove garlic, finely chopped
- dash of salt
- 7 oz (200 g) tomatoes, canned, drained and chopped
- 2 teaspoons parsley, finely chopped
- 6 leaves fresh basil, torn
- 5 oz (150 g) Pecorino cheese, diced

Wine: a dry white (Corvo di Salaparuta)

Calzone alle bietole
Swiss chard calzone

This is recipe comes from Basilicata, in the south. The region is known for its austere cuisine, which is livened up by the liberal use of hot chillies.

Makes: 4 calzoni; Preparation: 40 minutes; Rising time: about 1 hour; Cooking: 20-25 minutes; Level of difficulty: Medium

Prepare the dough as shown on pages 12–13. § Clean the Swiss chard, rinse thoroughly, drain well, and cut into strips. Place in a heavy-bottomed saucepan with 2–3 tablespoons of oil, the garlic, chillies, and salt to taste. Cook over medium-low heat, initially with the lid on, for 10 minutes, stirring from time to time. The Swiss chard should be tender but not watery. Add the

■ INGREDIENTS

BASE
- 3 quantities pizza dough (see recipe p. 14)

FILLING
- 1¾ lb (800 g) fresh Swiss chard (silver beet)
- 4 tablespoons extra-virgin olive oil

Right: Calzone alle melanzane

- 2 cloves garlic, sliced
- 1 teaspoon crushed chillies
- dash of salt
- 7 oz (200 g) black olives, pitted

*Wine: a dry white
(Bianco di Custoza)*

olives and cook for 2–4 minutes more. Set aside to cool. § When the rising time has elapsed, knead the dough for 1 minute on a lightly floured work surface, then divide into 4 equal portions. § Stretch the dough into circular shapes, about 9 in (23 cm) in diameter, as explained on page 14. § Spread the filling on one half of each calzone, leaving a ¾-in (2-cm) border around the edge for sealing. Fold the other half of the dough over the top, pressing down firmly on the edges to seal. § Brush the calzoni with the remaining oil, and arrange them on two lightly oiled baking sheets. § Bake in a preheated oven at 450°F/230°C/gas 7 for 20–25 minutes. § Serve hot.

VARIATION
– Add a few slices of Pecorino cheese or 2–3 tablespoons of freshly grated Parmesan to the filling.

Calzone alla pugliese
Apulian-style calzone

Makes: 4 calzoni; Preparation: 35 minutes; Rising time: about 1 hour; Cooking: 20-25 minutes;
Level of difficulty: Medium

Prepare the dough as shown on pages 12–13. § Cook the onions with 2–3 tablespoons of oil in a large sauté pan for 5 minutes. Add the tomatoes, olives, anchovies, capers, basil, and salt. Mix and cook over medium heat for 3–4 minutes more. Remove from heat. § When the mixture is cool, add the Pecorino. § When the rising time has elapsed, knead the dough on a lightly floured work surface, then divide into 4 equal portions. § Stretch the dough into circular shapes, about 9 in (23 cm) in diameter, as explained on page 14. § Spread the filling on one half of each calzone, leaving a ¾-in (2-cm) border around the edge for sealing. Fold the other half of the dough over the top, pressing down firmly on the edges to seal. § Brush the calzoni with the remaining oil, and arrange them on two lightly oiled baking sheets. § Bake in a preheated oven at 450°F/230°C/gas 7 for 20–25 minutes. § Serve hot.

Calzone al prosciutto e formaggi
Calzone with prosciutto and cheese

Makes: 4 calzoni; Preparation: 35 minutes; Rising time: about 1 hour; Cooking: 20-25 minutes;
Level of difficulty: Medium

Prepare the dough as shown on pages 12–13. § Combine the prosciutto, cheeses, and parsley in a bowl. Set aside. § When the rising time has elapsed, knead the dough for 1 minute on a lightly floured work surface, then divide into 4 equal portions. § Stretch the dough into circular shapes, about 9 in (23 cm) in diameter, as explained on page 14. § Spread the filling on one half of each calzone, leaving a ¾-in (2-cm) border around the edge. Fold the other half of the dough over the top, pressing down firmly on the edges to seal. § Brush the calzoni with the oil, and arrange them on two lightly oiled baking sheets. § Bake in a preheated oven at 450°F/230°C/gas 7 for 20–25 minutes. § Serve hot.

■ INGREDIENTS

BASE
• 3 quantities pizza dough (see recipe p. 14)

FILLING
• 1¼ lb (600 g) onions, sliced
• 4 tablespoons extra-virgin olive oil
• 8 oz (250 g) tomatoes, canned, drained, and chopped
• 7 oz (200 g) black olives, pitted and halved
• 8 anchovy fillets, crumbled
• 2 tablespoons capers
• 8 leaves fresh basil, torn
• dash of salt
• 4 oz (125 g) Pecorino cheese, diced

Wine: a dry rosé
(Castel del Monte)

■ INGREDIENTS

BASE
• 3 quantities pizza dough (see recipe p. 14)

FILLING
• 3½ oz (100 g) prosciutto, coarsely chopped
• 5 oz (150 g) Provolone, or Caciocavallo cheese, diced
• 5 oz (150 g) salted Ricotta cheese, freshly grated
• 5 oz (150 g) Mozzarella cheese, diced
• 1 tablespoon parsley, finely chopped
• 2 tablespoons extra-virgin olive oil

Wine: a dry white
(Bianco di Cervèteri)

Right: *Calzone alla pugliese*

BREAD

The variety of breads available in Italy is enormous. Each region
has developed its own special array of loaves and rolls. The recipes in
this chapter are a selection of some of the classics.

Pane Bianco
White bread

Basic breads like this one, made with flour, water, yeast, and salt, are best eaten the day they are made. If you make more than you can eat or give away, remember that this bread freezes very well. Wrap the bread tightly in plastic wrap, and place it in the freezer. Breads made with milk, olive oil, or butter will keep longer. Store them in a paper bag (not plastic) in a cool, dark place.

Makes: about 2 lb (1 kg) of bread; Preparation: 30 minutes; Rising time: about 2¼ hours; Cooking: 20-40 minutes; Level of difficulty: Medium

Prepare the yeast as explained on page 12. § Combine the flour in a large bowl with the yeast mixture, salt, and remaining water, and proceed as shown on pages 12–13. § When the rising time has elapsed (about 1½ hours), use a spatula to transfer the dough to a lightly floured work surface. Knead for several minutes. § Place the dough on an oiled baking sheet and shape it into an oval or elongated loaf. § Sprinkle the surface with flour and, using a serrated knife, make 5 or 6 diagonal slashes about ½ in (1 cm) deep along the top of the loaf. § For a large, ring-shaped loaf, about 12 in (30 cm) in diameter, gently flatten the dough and make a hole in the middle with your fingers. Carefully enlarge the hole, shaping the dough into a ring. § To make rolls, divide the dough into 8–10 equal portions and shape them into long rolls. Remember that the volume of the dough will double during rising, so position the rolls at least 1½ in (4 cm) apart. § Cover with a cloth and set aside to rise for 40–50 minutes. § Bake in a preheated oven at 450°F/230°C/gas 7. Large loaves will need about 40 minutes, the ring-shaped loaf about 30 minutes and the rolls about 25 minutes.

■ INGREDIENTS

- ¾ oz (25 g) fresh yeast or 1½ packages active dry yeast
- 1 teaspoon sugar
- about 1⅓ cups (12 fl oz/ 350 ml) lukewarm water
- 6 cups (7½ oz/750 g) unbleached white flour
- 2–4 teaspoons salt

VARIATIONS
— For loaves or rolls with golden crusts, instead of sprinkling the dough with flour, brush the surface with a lightly beaten egg (or 2 tablespoons of milk) before baking.
— For crispy rolls, sprinkle the dough with coarse-grain cornmeal before setting it aside to rise the second time.
— Shape the dough into long thin loaves, the thickness of your wrist. Sprinkle the surface with flour and, using a serrated knife, make an incision along the length of each loaf, or make several diagonal slashes. The loaves will take 20–25 minutes to cook.
— Add 2 tablespoons of fennel seeds to the dough for extra taste. Fresh, home-baked fennel bread should be served with a mixed platter of ham, prosciutto, mortadella, salami, and cheeses.

Right:
Pane bianco e pane all'olio

- ¾ oz (25 g) fresh yeast or 1½ packages active dry yeast
- 1 teaspoon sugar
- about 1¼ cups (10 fl oz/ 300 ml) lukewarm water
- 6 cups (7½ oz/750 g) unbleached white flour
- 2–4 teaspoons salt
- 4 tablespoons extra-virgin olive oil

Pane all'olio
Olive oil bread

Makes: about 2 lb (1 kg) of bread; Preparation: 30 minutes; Rising time: about 2 hours; Cooking: 35 minutes; Level of difficulty: Medium

Proceed as for white bread (see previous page), adding the oil to the yeast mixture at the beginning. Instead of kneading, mix the soft, sticky dough in the bowl with a wooden spoon. § When the rising time has elapsed (about 1½ hours), mix the dough again for a few minutes. § Use a spatula to transfer it to an oiled baking pan about 12 in (30 cm) in diameter. Cover with a cloth and set aside to rise for 30 minutes. § Bake in a preheated oven at 450°F/230°C/gas 7.

■ INGREDIENTS

- 3 oz (90 g) lard
- 1 oz (30 g) fresh yeast or 2 packages active dry yeast
- 1 teaspoon sugar
- about 1¼ cups (10 fl oz/ 300 ml) lukewarm water
- 6 cups (1½ lb/750 g) unbleached white flour
- 2–4 teaspoons salt

PANE ALLO STRUTTO
Bread made with lard

Makes: about 2 lb (1 kg) of bread; Preparation: 30 minutes; Rising time: about 2 hours; Cooking: 30-35 minutes; Level of difficulty: Medium

Melt the lard in a small saucepan over low heat. Remove from heat and set aside. § Prepare the yeast as explained on page 12. § Combine the flour in a large bowl with the lard, yeast mixture, salt, and remaining water, and proceed as shown on pages 12–13. § When the rising time has elapsed (about 1½ hours), use a spatula to transfer the dough to a lightly floured work surface and knead for several minutes. § Divide the dough into 6 equal portions and shape them into thin loaves about 12 in (30 cm) long. Pick each loaf up and twist it slightly, making sure it does not become too long. The loaves should have a very slight spiral shape. § As you finish twisting the loaves, place them on two oiled baking sheets, keeping them well spaced (their volume will double as they rise). § Cover with a cloth and set aside to rise for 30–40 minutes. § Bake in a preheated oven at 400°F/200°C/gas 6 for about 30–35 minutes.

PANE ALL'ORIGANO
Oregano bread

Makes: about 2 lb (1 kg) of bread; Preparation: 30 minutes; Rising time: about 2 hours; Cooking: 35 minutes; Level of difficulty: Medium

Prepare the yeast as explained on page 12. § Combine the flour in a large bowl with the oregano, yeast mixture, salt and remaining water, and proceed as shown on pages 12–13. § When the rising time has elapsed (about 1½ hours), use a spatula to transfer the dough to a lightly floured work surface. Knead for several minutes. § Divide the dough into 4–6 equal portions and shape each into a loaf about 14 in (35 cm) long. § Place the loaves on two oiled baking sheets. Pull the ends of each loaf round and join them to make circular loaves, or leave them straight, as preferred. § Use a serrated knife to make a ½-in (1-cm) deep incision along the top of each loaf. § Cover with a cloth and set aside to rise for 30–40 minutes. § Bake in a preheated oven at 400°F/200°C/gas 6 for about 30 minutes.

■ INGREDIENTS

- ¾ oz (25 g) fresh yeast or 1½ packages active dry yeast
- 1 teaspoon sugar
- about 1¼ cups (10 fl oz/ 300 ml) lukewarm water
- 6 cups (7½ oz/750 g) unbleached white flour
- 2 teaspoons fresh oregano, finely chopped
- 2–4 teaspoons salt
- ⅓ cup (3½ fl oz/100 ml) extra-virgin olive oil

Left: *Pane all'origano*

Pane integrale
Whole wheat bread

Makes: about 2 lb (1 kg) of bread; Preparation: 30 minutes; Rising time: 3-4 hours; Cooking: 40 minutes; Level of difficulty: Medium

Prepare the yeast as explained on page 12. § Combine both flours in a large bowl with the yeast mixture, salt, and remaining water, and proceed as shown on pages 12–13. § When the rising time has elapsed (about 2 hours), use a spatula to transfer the dough to a lightly floured work surface and knead for 5 minutes. § Divide the dough into two equal portions and shape each into a long loaf. Sprinkle with flour and use a serrated knife to make diagonal slashes about ¼ in (6 mm) deep along the top of each loaf. Repeat, making slashes in the other direction to create a grid pattern. § Cover with a cloth and set aside to rise for about 1½ hours. § Bake in a preheated oven at 400°F/200°C/gas 6 for 40 minutes.

> VARIATIONS
> – For a darker bread, increase the quantity of whole wheat flour, reducing the white flour proportionally.
> – Add 3–4 tablespoons of extra-virgin olive oil to the dough.

■ INGREDIENTS

- 1 oz (30 g) fresh yeast or 2 packages active dry yeast
- 1 teaspoon sugar
- about 1¼ cups (10 fl oz/ 300 ml) lukewarm water
- 3 cups (12 oz/350 g) whole wheat (wholemeal) flour
- 2¾ cups (10 oz/300 g) unbleached white flour
- 2–3 teaspoons salt

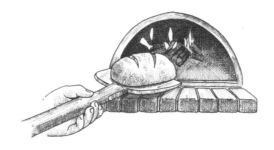

Pane al sesamo
Sesame seed bread

Sesame seed bread is made in Sicily in the south, where white loaves are sprinkled with the seeds before baking, and in Trento and Bolzano in the north. This recipe comes from the north.

Makes: about 2 lb (1 kg) of bread; Preparation: 30 minutes; Rising time: about 2 hours; Cooking: 30-40 minutes; Level of difficulty: Medium

Prepare the yeast as explained on page 12. § Combine both flours in a large bowl with half the sesame seeds. Mix carefully and sprinkle with salt. Add the yeast mixture and remaining water, and proceed as shown

■ INGREDIENTS

- 1 oz (30 g) fresh yeast or 2 packages active dry yeast
- 1 teaspoon sugar
- about 1¼ cups (10 fl oz/ 300 ml) lukewarm water
- 3½ cups (14 oz/450 g) unbleached white flour

Right: *Pane al sesamo*

- 2¾ cups (10 oz/300 g) whole wheat (wholemeal) flour
- 4 tablespoons sesame seeds
- 4 teaspoons salt
- 1 egg white

on pages 12–13. § When the rising time has elapsed (about 1 hour), use a spatula to transfer the dough to a lightly floured work surface and knead for 2–3 minutes. § Divide the dough into two equal portions to make soft loaves, or in 8–10 equal portions for crusty rolls. § Arrange the loaves or rolls on one or two oiled baking sheets, keeping them well spaced (their volume will double as they rise). § Lightly beat the egg white with 1 teaspoon of water and brush the surface of the loaves or rolls with the mixture. Sprinkle with the remaining sesame seeds. § Cover with a cloth and set aside to rise for 1 hour. § Bake in a preheated oven at 400°F/200°C/gas 6 for 35–40 minutes for loaves and 30 minutes for rolls.

■ INGREDIENTS

- 1 oz (30 g) fresh yeast or 2 packages active dry yeast
- 1 teaspoon sugar
- about 1¼ cups (10 fl oz/ 300 ml) lukewarm water
- 3½ cups (14 oz/450 g) rye flour
- 2 cups (7 oz/200 g) unbleached white flour
- 1 tablespoon fennel seeds
- 2 teaspoons salt
- 2 tablespoons extra-virgin olive oil or lard, at room temperature

PANE DI SEGALE
Rye bread

This tasty, fragrant bread comes from Alto Adige and Trentino in northeastern Italy.

Makes: about 2 lb (1 kg) of bread; Preparation: 30 minutes; Rising time: 2-3 hours; Cooking: 30 minutes; Level of difficulty: Medium

Prepare the yeast as explained on page 12. § Combine both flours in a large bowl with the fennel seeds, salt, yeast mixture, oil (or lard), and the remaining water, and proceed as shown on pages 12–13. § When the rising time has elapsed (about 2 hours), use a spatula to transfer the dough to a lightly floured work surface and knead for 2–3 minutes. The dough should be quite soft. § Divide the dough into 4–6 equal portions and shape into round loaves. Transfer to two oiled baking sheets. Cover with a cloth and set aside to rise for about 1 hour. § Bake in a preheated oven at 400°F/200°C/gas 6 for about 30 minutes.

■ INGREDIENTS

- ¾ oz (25 g) fresh yeast or 1½ packages active dry yeast
- 1 teaspoon sugar
- about 1 cup (8 fl oz/ 250 ml) lukewarm water
- 8 oz (250 g) garbanzo beans (chick peas), soaked and precooked, or canned
- 5 cups (1¼ lb/600 g) unbleached white flour
- 4 teaspoons salt
- 5 tablespoons extra-virgin olive oil

PANE CON CECI
Garbanzo bean rolls

Makes: about 16–20 rolls; Preparation: 30 minutes; Rising time: about 3 hours; Cooking: 18-20 minutes; Level of difficulty: Medium

Prepare the yeast as explained on page 12. § Drain the garbanzo beans and purée in a food processor with the remaining water. § Combine the flour in a large bowl with the salt, yeast mixture, garbanzo bean purée, and 4 tablespoons of oil, and proceed as shown on pages 12–13. § When the rising time has elapsed (at least 1½ hours), use a spatula to transfer the dough to a lightly floured work surface and knead for 2 minutes. § Divide the dough into 4 equal portions and shape into thin loaves about 14 in (35 cm) long. Divide each into 4 or 5 rolls. § Pour a few drops of the remaining oil on to each and spread it with your fingers while shaping the dough into round rolls. § Use a serrated knife to make a ¼ in (6 mm) deep cross in the surface of each roll. § Transfer to two oiled baking sheets, keeping the rolls well spaced (their volume will double as they rise). Cover with a cloth and set aside to rise for at least 1 hour. § Bake in a preheated oven at 400°F/ 200°C/gas 6 for 18–20 minutes.

Left: Pane di segale

Pane di mais
Corn bread

Makes: about 1½ lb (750 g) bread; Preparation: 30 minutes; Rising time: 1½ hours; Cooking: 30 minutes; Level of difficulty: Medium

Prepare the yeast as explained on page 12, using half the milk instead of water. § Combine both flours in a large bowl with the salt, egg, yeast mixture, and remaining milk, and proceed as shown on pages 12–13. § When the rising time has elapsed (about 1 hour), transfer the dough to a lightly floured work surface and knead for 2–3 minutes. § Divide the dough in half and shape into two round loaves. Sprinkle with flour and transfer to an oiled baking sheet. § Cover with a cloth and set aside to rise for about 30 minutes. § Bake in a preheated oven at 400°F/200°C/gas 6 for about 30 minutes.

■ INGREDIENTS

- 1½ oz (45 g) fresh yeast or 3 packages active dry yeast
- 1 teaspoon sugar
- about 1 cup (8 fl oz/ 250 ml) lukewarm milk
- 2¾ cups (10 oz/300 g) unbleached white flour
- 2¾ cups (10 oz/300 g) finely ground cornmeal
- 4 teaspoons salt
- 1 egg, lightly beaten

Pane di grano saraceno
Buckwheat bread

*Buckwheat flour is used only in a few parts of northern Italy.
It produces a delicious coarse-grain bread with a distinctive flavor.*

Makes: about 2 lb (1 kg) of bread; Preparation: 30 minutes; Rising time: 2 hours; Cooking: 30-35 minutes; Level of difficulty: Medium

Prepare the yeast as explained on page 12. § Combine both flours in a large bowl with the salt, yeast mixture, oil and remaining water, and proceed as shown on pages 12–13. § When the rising time has elapsed (about 1 hour), use a spatula to transfer the dough to a lightly floured work surface and knead for 2–3 minutes. § Divide the dough in 4 equal portions and shape into small round loaves. Sprinkle with flour and use a serrated knife to cut a ½-in (1-cm) deep cross in the surface of each loaf. § Transfer to one or two oiled baking sheets. Cover with a cloth and set aside to rise for 1 hour. § Bake in a preheated oven at 400°F/200°C/gas 6 for 30–35 minutes. § The loaves can also be cooked in two oiled and lightly floured rectangular loaf pans.

■ INGREDIENTS

- 1¼ oz (40 g) fresh yeast or 2½ packages active dry yeast
- 1 teaspoon sugar
- about 1⅓ cups (12 fl oz/ 350 ml) lukewarm water
- 4 cups (1 lb/500 g) buckwheat flour
- 2 cups (7 oz/200 g) unbleached white flour
- 3 teaspoons salt
- 4 tablespoons extra-virgin olive oil

Right:
Pane di mais

Pane alle noci
Walnut bread

This is a salted and not strictly traditional version of Pannociato *from the Marches region in central Italy. It is excellent for snacks and goes well with soft, fresh cheeses, such as Mascarpone and Robiola.*

Makes: about 2½ lb (1.2 kg) of bread; Preparation: 40 minutes; Rising time: 2 hours; Cooking: 25-30 minutes; Level of difficulty: Medium

Prepare the yeast as explained on page 12. § Combine the flour, Pecorino, walnuts, salt, and pepper in a large bowl. Mix well and add the lard (or oil), yeast mixture, and remaining water, and proceed as shown on pages 12–13. § When the rising time has elapsed (about 1 hour), transfer the dough to a lightly floured work surface and knead for 2–3 minutes. § Divide into 8–10 equal portions and shape into long rolls. § Place on two oiled baking sheets, keeping them well spaced (their volume will double as they rise). § Cover with a cloth and set aside to rise for about 1 hour. § Bake in a preheated oven at 400°F/200°C/gas 6 for 25–30 minutes.

■ INGREDIENTS

- 1 oz (30 g) fresh yeast or 2 packages active dry yeast
- 1 teaspoon sugar
- about 1¼ cups (10 fl oz/ 300 ml) lukewarm water
- 4 cups (1 lb/500 g) unbleached white flour
- 5 oz (150 g) Pecorino cheese, diced
- 1¼ cups (5 oz/150 g) walnuts, shelled and coarsely chopped
- 3 teaspoons salt
- freshly ground black pepper
- 2 tablespoons lard, at room temperature, or 3 tablespoons extra-virgin olive oil

Pane integrale con nocciole
Whole wheat bread with hazelnuts

The distinctive nutty taste of this bread goes very well with fresh, creamy cheeses.

Makes: about 2 lb (1 kg) of bread; Preparation: 30 minutes; Rising time: 2 hours; Cooking: 30 minutes; Level of difficulty: Medium

Prepare the yeast as explained on page 12. § Combine both flours in a large bowl with the hazelnuts, mix well and sprinkle with salt. Add the yeast mixture, 3 tablespoons of oil, and the remaining water, and proceed as shown on pages 12–13. § When the rising time has elapsed (about 1 hour), use a spatula to transfer the dough (which will be very soft) to a lightly floured work surface and knead for 2–3 minutes. § Grease a nonstick baking pan 12 in (30 cm) in diameter with the remaining oil and place the dough in it. Cover with a cloth and set aside to rise for 1 hour. § Bake in a preheated oven at 400°F/200°C/gas 6 for about 30 minutes.

■ INGREDIENTS

- 1 oz (30 g) fresh yeast or 2 packages active dry yeast
- 1 teaspoon sugar
- about 1¼ cups (10 fl oz/ 300 ml) lukewarm water
- 4 cups (1 lb/500 g) whole wheat (wholemeal) flour
- 2 cups (7 oz/200 g) unbleached white flour
- ¾ cup (3 oz/90 g) roasted hazelnuts, shelled and coarsely chopped
- 3 teaspoons salt
- 4 tablespoons extra-virgin olive oil

VARIATIONS
– For softer bread, increase the quantity of water by 3 tablespoons and use a wooden spoon to mix the dough in the bowl instead of kneading it.
– For darker, drier bread, replace the white flour with whole wheat (wholemeal) flour.

Right: *Pane alle noci*

Pane con patate
Potato rolls

■ INGREDIENTS

- ¾ oz (25 g) fresh yeast or 1½ packages active dry yeast
- 1 teaspoon sugar
- about ¾ cup (7 fl oz/ 200 ml) lukewarm water
- 5 oz (150 g) boiled potatoes, still warm
- 2 tablespoons extra-virgin olive oil
- 4 cups (1 lb/500 g) unbleached white flour
- 3 teaspoons salt

Makes: about 2 lb (1 kg) of bread; Preparation: 30 minutes; Rising time: 2 hours; Cooking: 25-30 minutes; Level of difficulty: Medium

Prepare the yeast as explained on page 12. § Mash the potatoes in a large bowl and stir in the oil, flour, salt, yeast mixture, and remaining water. Proceed as shown on pages 12–13. § When the rising time has elapsed, transfer the dough to a floured work surface and knead for 1 minute. § Divide into 4–6 equal portions and shape into rolls. § Place on oiled baking sheets, keeping well spaced. Cover with a cloth and set aside to rise for 45 minutes. § Bake in a preheated oven at 400°F/200°C/gas 6 for 25–30 minutes.

Pan di ramerino
Rosemary and raisin rolls

This recipe comes from Tuscany, where rosemary is often called ramerino. *Traditionally served during Lent, these delicious rolls are ideal for snacks and picnics all year round.*

Makes: about 1¼ lb (600 g) bread; Preparation: 30 minutes; Rising time: 1½ hours; Cooking: 20 minutes; Level of difficulty: Medium

Combine 1½ tablespoons of rosemary with 4 tablespoons of oil in a small pan and cook over low heat for about 10 minutes. Remove from heat, discard the rosemary, and set the oil aside to cool. § Prepare the yeast as explained on page 12. § Combine the flour in a large bowl with the salt, rosemary oil, yeast mixture, sugar, and remaining water, and proceed as shown on pages 12–13. § When the rising time has elapsed (about 1 hour), transfer the dough to a lightly floured work surface and knead for 2–3 minutes. Incorporate the raisins and remaining rosemary into the dough as you knead. § Divide in 6–8 equal portions, drizzle with the remaining oil and shape into oval rolls. § Place on an oiled baking sheet, keeping them well spaced. Use a serrated knife to make a ½-in (1-cm) deep cross in the surface of each roll. § Cover with a cloth and set aside to rise for 30 minutes. § Bake in a preheated oven at 400°F/200°C/gas 6 for 20 minutes.

■ INGREDIENTS

- 2 tablespoons fresh rosemary leaves
- 5 tablespoons extra-virgin olive oil
- ½ oz (15 g) fresh yeast or 1 package active dry yeast
- 2 teaspoons sugar
- ⅔ cup (5 fl oz/150 ml) lukewarm water
- 3 cups (12 oz/350 g) unbleached white flour
- 2 teaspoons salt
- ⅔ cup (2½ oz/75 g) raisins, rinsed, drained, and dried

Pane con l'uva
Raisin bread

This is a very old recipe, common to many parts of Italy. The raisins and sugar make it slightly sweet. Serve with Mascarpone or another mild, creamy cheese.

Makes: about 1¾ lb (800 g) of bread; Preparation: 30 minutes; Rising time: 1½ hours; Cooking: 20 minutes; Level of difficulty: Medium

Prepare the yeast as explained on page 12. § Combine the flour in a large bowl with the remaining sugar and water, the salt and yeast mixture, and proceed as shown on pages 12–13. § Soak the raisins in 2 cups of lukewarm water for 15–20 minutes. Drain, dry, and lightly sprinkle with flour. § When the rising time has elapsed (about 1 hour), transfer the dough to a lightly floured work surface and knead. Incorporate the raisins and butter into the dough as you knead. § Divide in 7–8 equal portions, sprinkle with flour and shape into long rolls. § Place on an oiled baking sheet, keeping them well spaced. Cover with a cloth and set aside to rise for about 30 minutes. § Bake in a preheated oven at 400°F/200°C/gas 6 for about 20 minutes.

■ INGREDIENTS

- ¾ oz (25 g) fresh yeast or 1½ packages active dry yeast
- 2 tablespoons sugar
- ⅔ cup (5 fl oz/150 ml) lukewarm water
- 3 cups (12 oz/350 g) unbleached white flour
- 2½ tablespoons butter, at room temperature, chopped into small pieces
- 1½ cups (6 oz/180 g) Malaga (or Corinth) raisins
- 2 teaspoons salt

Right:

Pan di ramerino

Tarallucci
Breadrings

Taralluci are a speciality of southern Italy. This version comes from Apulia, the so-called "heel" of the Italian peninsula. These small, breadrings can be seasoned with fennel seeds, chillies, or lard. They make perfect appetizers and snacks.

Makes: about 65 breadrings; Preparation: 1½ hours; Cooking: 35 minutes; Level of difficulty: Medium

Combine the flour in a large bowl with the salt, oil, and wine. Mix well with a fork until all the flour has been absorbed. § Use a spatula to transfer the dough to a lightly floured work surface. Knead as shown on page 343 until the dough is soft, smooth, and elastic. § Return to the bowl and set aside for 20 minutes. § Divide the dough into 8–10 equal portions and shape each one into a long roll about the thickness of your little finger. The dough will be very elastic and tend to contract; wet your hands so that you can work more easily. § Divide each roll into segments about 3 in (8 cm) long. Using your fingers and thumb, pinch the ends of each segment together to form a ring. Place the breadrings on paper towels. § Bring a large pan containing about 3 quarts (6 pints/3 liters) of salted water to a boil. Add the tarallucci (not more than 20 at a time), and boil until they rise to the surface. Scoop them out with a slotted spoon and place them on three or four oiled baking sheets. § Cover with lightly oiled foil and set aside to dry for about 30 minutes. § Bake in a preheated oven at 400°F/200°C/gas 6 for 20–25 minutes.

> VARIATIONS
> – Replace the oil with the same quantity of melted and slightly cooled lard.
> – Add 3 teaspoons of freshly ground black pepper, or a heaped tablespoon of fennel seeds, or 3 teaspoons of crushed chillies to the flour.

■ INGREDIENTS

- 4 cups (1 lb /500 g) unbleached white flour
- 4 tablespoons extra-virgin olive oil
- about 1 cup (8 fl oz/ 250 ml) dry white wine
- 2 teaspoons salt

Grissini
Breadsticks

Makes: about 16 oz (500 g) breadsticks; Preparation: 30 minutes; Rising time: 2 hours; Cooking: 4-5 minutes; Level of difficulty: Medium

Prepare the yeast as explained on page 12. § Combine the flour in a large bowl with the salt, yeast mixture, and remaining water, and proceed as shown on pages 12–13. § When the rising time has elapsed (about 1 hour), transfer the dough to a lightly floured work surface and knead for 2–3 minutes. § Divide

■ INGREDIENTS

- ¾ oz (25 g) fresh yeast or 1½ packages active dry yeast
- 1 teaspoon sugar
- about ¾ cup (7 fl oz/ 200 ml) lukewarm water
- 3½ cups (14 oz/450 g) unbleached white flour
- 1 teaspoon salt

the dough into portions about the size of an egg, then shape them into sticks about the thickness of your little finger. § Sprinkle with flour and transfer to three oiled baking sheets, keeping them a finger's width apart. § Cover with a cloth and set aside to rise for 1 hour. § Bake in a preheated oven at 450°F/230°C/gas 7 for 5 minutes. When cooked, the breadsticks should be well-browned. Leave to cool before removing from the sheets.

Above:

Taralluci and Grissini

VARIATIONS
– Use whole wheat flour instead of white, or a mixture of the two.
– Add 3 tablespoons of extra-virgin olive oil to the dough. Reduce the amount of water proportionally.
– Increase the amount of yeast to 1 oz (30 g) fresh yeast, or 2 packages of active dry yeast.
– Replace the water partly or entirely with milk.

PANE AL FORMAGGIO
Parmesan bread

Makes: about 2 lb (1 kg) of bread; Preparation: 30 minutes; Rising time: 2 hours; Cooking: 30 minutes; Level of difficulty: Medium

Prepare the yeast as explained on page 12. § Combine the flour in a large bowl with the cheese and pepper, if liked. Mix well, sprinkle with salt, and add the yeast mixture and remaining water. Proceed as shown on pages 12–13. § When the rising time has elapsed (about 1 hour), transfer the dough to a lightly floured work surface and knead for 2 minutes. § Divide the dough into 4 equal portions and shape each into a roll about 16 in (40 cm) long. Brush each roll with the egg. Sprinkle two rolls with poppy seeds and two with sesame seeds. § Fold each roll in two, twisting the two parts of each carefully, to make a false braid. § Transfer to two oiled baking sheets. § Cover with a cloth and set aside to rise for 1 hour. § Bake in a preheated oven at 400°F/200°C/gas 6 for 30 minutes.

VARIATIONS
– Replace the water partly or entirely with milk.
– Replace the Parmesan with the same quantity of another tasty cheese.
– Add 3 tablespoons of extra-virgin olive oil to the dough, reducing the amount of water proportionally.

■ INGREDIENTS

• ¾ oz (25 g) fresh yeast or 1½ packages active dry yeast
• 1 teaspoon sugar
• about 1¼ cups (10 fl oz/ 300 ml) lukewarm water
• 5 cups (1¼ lb/600 g) unbleached white flour
• 2 cups (8 oz/250 g) Parmesan cheese, freshly grated
• freshly ground white pepper (optional)
• 2 teaspoons salt
• 1 egg, lightly beaten
• 2 tablespoons poppy seeds
• 2 tablespoons sesame seeds

PIADINE
Unleavened bread, Emilia-Romagna-style

This small, thin focaccia is traditionally charcoal-grilled on a red hot testo, *a slab of heatproof clay.*

Makes: about 10 piadine; Preparation: 1 hour; Cooking: 30 minutes; Level of difficulty: Medium

Combine the flour in a large bowl with the salt. Make a hollow in the flour and add the lard and water. Mix well, then transfer to a lightly floured work surface. § Knead until the dough is smooth and elastic. Return to the bowl. Cover with a cloth and set aside for about 30 minutes. § Knead again for 1 minute. § Divide into pieces about the size of an egg. Sprinkle with flour and roll into ⅛-in (3-mm) thick round shapes about 6 in (15 cm) in diameter. Prick well with a fork. § Cook one at a time in a very hot iron or cast-iron pan, without adding any fat. After 2–3 minutes, turn the piadine and cook for 2–3 minutes more. § Stack the piadine up on a plate and serve hot with cured meats and fresh, soft cheeses.

■ INGREDIENTS

• 3 cups (12 oz/350 g) unbleached white flour
• ⅓ cup (3½ oz/100 g) lard, at room temperature, thinly sliced
• about ½ cup (4 fl oz/ 125 ml) lukewarm water
• 1 teaspoon salt

Right: *Piadine*

FOCACCE

Salty or sweet, leavened or unleavened, focaccia is as old as bread itself. It is made in a huge variety of ways, depending on local ingredients and traditions.

Focaccia all'olio
Focaccia with oil

Liguria is famous for the quality of its many focacce. This is the basic recipe; several variations follow. Focacce *can be served hot, warm, or cold; they are always delicious.*

Makes: 1 focaccia, about 12 in (30 cm) in diameter; Preparation: 20 minutes; Rising time: 1½ hours; Cooking: 20 minutes; Level of difficulty: Medium

Prepare the yeast as explained on page 12. § Combine the flour in a large bowl with the fine salt, yeast mixture, 3 tablespoons of oil, and the remaining water, and proceed as shown in the sequence on pages 12–13. § When the rising time has elapsed (about 1½ hours), transfer the dough to a lightly floured work surface and knead for 2–3 minutes. § Place the dough on an oiled baking sheet and, using your hands, spread it into a circular shape about 12 in (30 cm) in diameter and ½ in (1 cm) thick. Dimple the surface with your fingertips, drizzle with the remaining oil, and sprinkle with the coarse salt. § Bake in a preheated oven at 450°F/230°C/gas 7 for about 20 minutes. The focaccia should be well-browned but soft. The bottoms of the dimples in the surface should be light gold.

> VARIATIONS
> – Use a rolling pin to flatten and spread the dough at first, then complete the process by hand.
> – Spread the dough in an oiled, rectangular nonstick pan. The crisp corner pieces are especially good.
> – After spreading the dough into a circular shape, sprinkle the surface evenly with a little flour.

INGREDIENTS
- ½ oz (15 g) fresh yeast or 1 package active dry yeast
- 1 teaspoon sugar
- about ¾ cup (7 fl oz/ 200 ml) lukewarm water
- 3 cups (12 oz/350 g) unbleached white flour
- 1 teaspoon salt
- ⅓ cups (3½ fl oz/100 ml) extra-virgin olive oil
- 1 teaspoon coarse salt

Wine: a light, dry white (Soave)

Focaccia al rosmarino
Rosemary focaccia

Makes 1 focaccia, about 12 in (30 cm) in diameter; Preparation: 20 minutes; Rising time: 1½ hours; Cooking: 20 minutes; Level of difficulty: Medium

Prepare the focaccia as explained in the recipe above. § Incorporate the rosemary into the dough as you knead after the second rising. § Alternatively, instead of chopping the rosemary leaves, sprinkle them whole over the surface of the dough when spread.

INGREDIENTS
- 1 quantity dough for *Focaccia all'olio* (see recipe above)
- 1 tablespoon fresh rosemary, finely chopped

Wine: a dry white (Frascati)

Right: *Focaccia al rosmarino*

Focaccia alla salvia
Sage focaccia

Makes 1 focaccia, about 12 in (30 cm) in diameter; Preparation: 20 minutes; Rising time: 1½ hours; Cooking: 20 minutes; Level of difficulty: Medium

Prepare the focaccia as described in the recipe on page 74. § Incorporate the sage into the dough as you knead after the second rising. § Alternatively, sauté the sage in 1 tablespoon of olive oil over medium heat for 1 minute before adding. In this case, reduce the amount of oil added to the flour by 1 tablespoon.

■ INGREDIENTS
- 1 quantity dough for *Focaccia all'olio* (see recipe p. 74)
- 1 heaped tablespoon fresh sage leaves, coarsely chopped

Wine: a dry white (Pigato)

Focaccia con olive nere
Focaccia with black olives

Makes 1 focaccia, about 12 in (30 cm) in diameter; Preparation: 20 minutes; Rising time: 1½ hours; Cooking: 20 minutes; Level of difficulty: Medium

Prepare the focaccia as described in the recipe on page 74. § Incorporate the olives into the dough as you knead after the second rising.

■ INGREDIENTS
- 1 quantity dough for *Focaccia all'olio* (see recipe p. 74)
- 7 oz (200 g) black olives, pitted and coarsely chopped

Wine: a light, dry red (Lambrusco)

Focaccia con olive verdi
Focaccia with green olives

Makes: 1 focaccia, about 12 in (30 cm) in diameter; Preparation: 20 minutes; Rising time: 1½ hours; Cooking: 20 minutes; Level of difficulty: Medium

Prepare the focaccia as described in the recipe on page 74. § When the focaccia is ready, arrange the olives face down on the dough. Press them down with your fingers to make them sink into the dough a little.

■ INGREDIENTS
- 1 quantity dough for *Focaccia all'olio* (see recipe p. 74)
- (4 oz/125 g) green olives, pitted, and cut in half

Wine: a dry white (Pinot Bianco)

Focaccia al formaggio
Cheese focaccia

Makes: 1 focaccia, about 12 in (30 cm) in diameter; Preparation: 20 minutes; Rising time: 1½ hours; Cooking: 20 minutes; Level of difficulty: Medium

Prepare the focaccia as described in the recipe for on page 74. § When the focaccia is ready, arrange the slices of cheese on top and bake.

■ INGREDIENTS
- 1 quantity dough for *Focaccia all'olio* (see recipe p. 74)
- 7 oz (200 g) Fontina cheese, or similar, cut in thin slices

Right: *Focaccia con olive verdi, Focaccia alla salvia, Focaccia al formaggio*

FOCACCIA CON CIPOLLA
Onion focaccia

■ INGREDIENTS

• 1 quantity dough for
  Focaccia all'olio (see recipe
  p. 74)
• 1 large white onion

Wine: a dry white
(Corvo)

*Makes 1 focaccia, about 12 in (30 cm) in diameter; Preparation: 20 minutes; Rising time: 1½
hours; Cooking: 20 minutes; Level of difficulty: Medium*

Prepare the focaccia as described in the recipe on page 74. § Cook the
onion in a pot of boiling, salted water for 3–4 minutes. Drain well, cut
into fairly thick slices, and spread over the surface of the focaccia
before sprinkling with the salt and drizzling with the oil.

- ¾ oz (25 g) fresh yeast or 1½ packages active dry yeast
- 1 teaspoon sugar
- ¾ cup (7 fl oz/200 ml) lukewarm water
- 1 cup (3½ oz/100 g) unbleached white flour
- 2½ cups (8 oz/250 g) whole wheat (wholemeal) flour
- 2 teaspoons salt
- 4 tablespoons extra-virgin olive oil
- 3½ oz (100 g) black olives, pitted and thinly sliced
- 2 fresh green chillies, thinly sliced

- ½ oz (15 g) fresh yeast or 1 package active dry yeast
- 1 teaspoon sugar
- about ⅔ cup (5 fl oz/150 ml) lukewarm water
- 2¾ cups (10 oz/300 g) unbleached white flour
- 1 teaspoon salt
- 10 oz (300 g) fresh, creamy cheese, such as Robiola or Crescenza
- ⅓ cup (3½ fl oz/100 ml) extra-virgin olive oil

Wine: a dry white (Vermentino)

FOCACCIA INTEGRALE
Whole wheat focaccia

Makes: 1 focaccia, about 12 in (30 cm) in diameter; Preparation: 30 minutes; Rising time: about 1½ hours; Cooking: 25 minutes; Level of difficulty: Medium

Prepare the yeast as explained on page 12. § Combine both flours in a large bowl with the salt, yeast mixture, 3 tablespoons of oil and the remaining water, and proceed as shown in the sequence on pages 12–13. § When the rising time has elapsed (about 1½ hours), transfer the dough to a lightly floured work surface and knead for 2-3 minutes. § Place the dough on an oiled baking sheet and, using your hands, spread it into a circular shape about 12 in (30 cm) in diameter and ½ in (1 cm) thick. Sprinkle with the olives and chillies, pressing them lightly into the dough with your fingertips. Drizzle with the remaining oil. § Bake in a preheated oven at 400°F/200°C/gas 6 for 25 minutes.

FOCACCIA DI RECCO
Focaccia filled with creamy cheese

The wonderful focaccia comes from Recco, near the city of Genoa in the northwest.

Makes: 1 focaccia about 13 in (32 cm) in diameter; Preparation: 30 minutes; Rising time: about 1½ hours; Cooking: 15 minutes; Level of difficulty: Medium

Prepare the yeast as explained on page 12. § Combine the flour in a large bowl with the salt, yeast mixture, 2 tablespoons of oil and the remaining water, and proceed as shown in the sequence on pages 12–13. § When the rising time has elapsed (about 1½ hours), transfer the dough to a lightly floured work surface and knead for 2–3 minutes. § Divide into two portions, one slightly larger than the other, and roll them out. The larger portion should be about 14 in (35 cm) in diameter, the smaller about 13 in (32 cm). § Transfer the larger one to an oiled baking sheet. Spread with the cheese, leaving a ¾-in (2-cm) border around the edge. § Cover with the smaller piece of dough. Fold back the edges of the larger sheet and press with your fingers to seal thoroughly. Prick several holes in the surface with a fork and brush with the remaining oil. § Bake in a preheated oven at 500°F/250°C/gas 8 for 15 minutes.

Left: Focaccia integrale

Fitascetta

Focaccia with onions

This is a regional recipe from the city of Como, in Lombardy, where it is made with the same dough as the renowned local bread.

■ INGREDIENTS

• ¾ oz (25 g) fresh yeast or 1½ packages active dried yeast

• 1 teaspoon sugar

• about ¾ cup (7 fl oz/ 200 ml) lukewarm water

• 3 cups (12 oz/350 g) unbleached white flour

• 2 teaspoons salt

• 1 lb (500 g) red onions

• 2 tablespoons butter

Wine: a dry red (Oltrepò Pavese)

Makes: 1 round focaccia, about 12 in (30 cm) in diameter; Preparation: 30 minutes; Rising time: 1½ hours; Cooking: 30 minutes; Level of difficulty: Medium

Prepare the yeast as explained on page 12. § Combine the flour in a large bowl with the salt, yeast mixture and remaining water, and proceed as shown in the sequence on pages 12–13. The dough should be rather soft; if it is difficult to knead, leave it in the bowl and mix for several minutes with a wooden spoon. § While the dough is rising, peel and slice the onions. Cook over medium-low heat with the butter and 2 tablespoons of water for 30 minutes. Remove from heat and leave to cool. § When the rising time has elapsed (about 1 hour), transfer the dough to a lightly floured work surface and knead for 2–3 minutes. § Shape into a loaf about 3 ft (1 m) long. § Transfer the loaf to an oiled baking sheet, and shape it into a ring, joining the two ends together, and leaving a large hole in the middle. § Cover with a cloth and set aside to rise for about 30 minutes. § When the second rising time has elapsed, flatten the dough a little with your hands and spread the onions on top. Sprinkle with salt. § Bake in a preheated oven at 400°F/200°C/gas 6 for about 30 minutes. § Serve hot.

VARIATIONS
– If you are short of time, omit the second rising time and put the fitasecca directly into the oven as soon as you switch it on. Lengthen cooking time by 10 minutes.
– For a sweet focaccia, omit the salt and sprinkle the onions with 1 tablespoon of sugar.
– Purists disapprove, but there is an excellent variation in which 7 oz (200 g) of thinly sliced fresh cheese is placed on top of the onions. Because the cheese will melt during cooking and will probably drip, spread the dough into a 1-in (2.5-cm) thick circular shape, rather than a ring. Leave a narrow border around the edge without topping. Cooking time will be shortened by several minutes.

Right: *Fitascetta*

PUDDICA

Focaccia with tomato and garlic

A fragrant focaccia from the Apulia region, in the south.

Makes: 1 focaccia, 12 in (30 cm) in diameter; Preparation: 30 minutes; Rising time: about 1½ hours; Cooking: 20-25 minutes; Level of difficulty: Medium

Prepare the yeast as explained on page 12. § Combine the flour in a large bowl with the salt, yeast mixture, 2 tablespoons of oil and the remaining water, and proceed as shown in the sequence on pages 12–13. § To peel the tomatoes, plunge them into a pot of boiling water for 30 seconds and then into cold. Slip off the skins, cut in half, and squeeze to remove some of the seeds. § When the rising time has elapsed (about 1½ hours), transfer the dough to a lightly floured work surface and knead for 1 minute. § Place on an oiled baking sheet, or in an oiled, nonstick rectangular baking pan and spread with your hands. § Dimple the surface with your fingertips and fill the dimples with pieces of garlic and tomato. § Drizzle the surface with the remaining oil and sprinkle with oregano and pepper. § Bake in a preheated oven at 450°F/230°C/gas 7 for 20–25 minutes. § Serve hot, warm or at room temperature.

■ INGREDIENTS

- ½ oz (15 g) fresh yeast or 1 package active dry yeast
- 1 teaspoon sugar
- ¾ cup (7 fl oz/200 ml) lukewarm water
- 3 cups (12 oz/350 g) unbleached white flour
- 1 teaspoon salt
- 4 tablespoons extra-virgin olive oil
- 6 small ripe tomatoes
- 3 cloves garlic, cut vertically in 4
- 2 teaspoons oregano
- freshly ground black pepper

Wine: a dry white (Locorotondo)

FOCACCIA CON PATATE

Focaccia with potatoes

This soft, delicious focaccia is always a great success.
It will keep for at least 3 days.

Makes: 1 focaccia, about 12 in (30 cm) in diameter; Preparation: 30 minutes; Rising time: 1½ hours; Cooking: 20-25 minutes; Level of difficulty: Medium

Prepare the yeast as explained on page 12. Use all the water to dissolve the yeast. § Mash the boiled potatoes while still hot. § Combine the potatoes in a large bowl with the flour, fine salt, yeast mixture and 1 tablespoon of oil, and proceed as shown in the sequence on pages 12–13. The dough will be too soft to knead by hand; leave it in the bowl and mix vigorously with a

■ INGREDIENTS

- ½ oz (15 g) fresh yeast or 1 package active dry yeast
- 1 teaspoon sugar
- about 4 tablespoons lukewarm water
- 8 oz (250 g) boiled potatoes, still warm

Right: Puddica

- 2½ cups (8 oz/250 g) unbleached white flour
- 2 teaspoons fine salt
- 4 tablespoons extra-virgin olive oil
- 1 teaspoon coarse salt

Wine: a dry white
(Roero Arneis)

wooden spoon for 2–3 minutes. Set aside to rise. § When the rising time has elapsed (about 1 hour), mix again for 1 minute. § Transfer to an oiled nonstick baking pan 12 in (30 cm) in diameter. Spread the dough with your hands. Cover with a cloth and set aside to rise for 30 minutes. § Sprinkle with the coarse salt. Dimple the surface with your fingertips and drizzle with the remaining oil. § Bake in a preheated oven at 400°F/200°C/gas 6 for 20–25 minutes. § Serve hot or at room temperature.

VARIATION
– Shape the dough into small focacce (*focaccette*) about 6 in (15 cm) in diameter and ¾ in (2 cm) thick. They will take 15–20 minutes to cook. Serve hot, or reheat briefly in the oven before serving.

FILLED BREADS AND PIES

Many of the recipes in this chapter are from southern
Italian cuisine. Hearty and rustic, they make wonderful
light lunches or picnic dishes.

PITTA ALLA CALABRESE
Calabrian-style filled bread

Makes: 1 filled bread, about 9 in (23 cm) in diameter; Preparation: 40 minutes; Rising time: about 2 hours; Cooking: 30 minutes; Level of difficulty: Medium

Prepare the dough as explained on pages 12–13, using the first 5 ingredients listed for the dough. § For the filling, combine the tomatoes, garlic, and half the oil in a saucepan. Cook over medium-low heat for 8–10 minutes, stirring frequently. Remove from heat and leave to cool. § Add the tuna, olives, anchovies, and capers. Mix well and taste before seasoning with salt and pepper. § When the rising time has elapsed (about 1½ hours), knead the dough on a lightly floured work surface for half a minute. Flatten the dough and spread with the lard. Add the egg yolk and knead again. § Break off about a third of the dough and set aside. § Roll the rest into a disk about 12 in (30 cm) in diameter. § Oil a 9-in (23-cm) springform pan and line the bottom and sides with the dough. § Spread with the filling. § Roll the remaining dough into a disk as large as the springform pan and cover the filling. Seal the dish by folding the edges of the first sheet of dough over the top sheet to make a border. § Brush the surface with oil, cover with a cloth, and set aside to rise for 30 minutes. § Bake in a preheated oven at 400°F/200°C/gas 6 for 30 minutes. Serve hot.

■ INGREDIENTS

DOUGH
- ½ oz (15 g) fresh yeast or 1 package active dry yeast
- 1 teaspoon sugar
- about ¾ cup (7 fl oz/200 ml) lukewarm water
- 3 cups (12 oz/350 g) unbleached white flour
- 2 teaspoons salt
- ¼ cup (2 oz/60 g) lard (or butter), at room temperature
- 1 egg yolk

FILLING
- 10 oz (300 g) tomatoes, peeled and chopped
- 1 clove garlic, finely chopped
- 4 tablespoons extra-virgin olive oil
- 1¼ cups (8 oz/250 g) tuna in oil, drained, and chopped
- ¾ cup (3 oz/90 g) black olives, pitted (stoned), cut in quarters
- 8 anchovy fillets, crumbled
- 1 tablespoon capers
- salt and freshly ground black pepper

Wine: a dry red (Savuto)

PITTA ALLA REGGINA
Filled bread with Ricotta and sausage

Makes: 1 filled bread, about 9 in (23 cm) in diameter; Preparation: 40 minutes; Rising time: about 2 hours; Cooking: 30 minutes; Level of difficulty: Medium

Prepare the dough as explained on pages 12–13, adding the oil to the flour. § Mix the Ricotta, sausage, Pecorino, parsley, salt, and pepper in a bowl. § When the rising time has elapsed (about 1¾ hours), knead the dough on a lightly floured work surface for half a minute. § Break off about a third of the dough and set aside. § Roll the rest into a disk about 12 in (30 cm) in diameter. Grease a 9-in (23-cm) springform pan with a little of the lard and

■ INGREDIENTS

DOUGH
- ½ oz (15 g) fresh yeast or 1 package active dry yeast
- 1 teaspoon sugar
- about ¾ cup (7 fl oz/200 ml) lukewarm water
- 3 cups (12 oz/350 g) unbleached white flour
- 3 tablespoons extra-virgin olive oil
- 2 teaspoons salt

Right: Pitta alla Reggina

FILLING
- 1 cup (8 oz/250 g) soft
  Ricotta cheese
- 4 oz (125 g) Italian
  sausage, crumbled
- 4 tablespoons Pecorino
  cheese, freshly grated
- 1 tablespoon parsley,
  finely chopped
- salt and freshly ground
  black pepper
- 2 hard-cooked (hard-
  boiled) eggs, sliced
- 1 tablespoon lard

line the base and sides with the dough. § Spread with half the filling, followed by a layer of egg. Cover with the rest of the filling. § Roll the remaining dough into a disk as large as the springform pan and cover the filling. Seal the dish by folding the edges of the first sheet of dough over the second to make a border. Prick the surface with a fork and dot with the remaining lard. Cover with a cloth and set aside in a warm place for 30 minutes. § Bake in a preheated oven at 400°F/200°C/gas 6 for 30 minutes. § Serve hot or at room temperature.

VARIATION
– Replace the sausage with the same quantity of prosciutto cut in a single, thick slice, and diced into cubes.

■ INGREDIENTS

DOUGH
- ½ oz (15 g) fresh yeast or 1 package active dry yeast
- 1 teaspoon sugar
- ¾ cup (7 fl oz/200 ml) lukewarm water
- 3 cups (12 oz/350 g) unbleached white flour
- 2 teaspoons salt
- 1 tablespoon lard, thinly sliced

FILLING
- 10 oz (300 g) Pecorino cheese, sliced
- 10 oz (300 g) ripe tomatoes
- salt and freshly ground black pepper
- 8 anchovy fillets, crumbled
- 2 tablespoons onion, finely chopped
- 1 tablespoon lard, chopped
- 1 tablespoon extra-virgin olive oil

Wine: a dry red (Cirò Rosso)

■ INGREDIENTS

- ¾ oz (25 g) fresh yeast, or 1½ packages active dry yeast
- 3½ tablespoons warm water
- 1 teaspoon sugar
- 3 eggs + 1 yolk, beaten
- ⅓ cup (3½ fl oz/100 ml) extra-virgin olive oil
- 2¾ cups (10 oz/300 g) unbleached white flour
- 8 oz (250 g) Parmesan cheese, freshly grated
- 2 teaspoons salt
- ½ teaspoon white pepper

Wine: a dry rosé (Brindisi Rosato)

Left: *Torta al formaggio*

Scacciata
Filled bread with Pecorino, tomato, and anchovies

Makes: 1 filled bread, about 9 in (23 cm) in diameter; Preparation: 35 minutes; Rising time: about 2 hours; Cooking: 30 minutes; Level of difficulty: Medium

Prepare the dough as explained on pages 12–13, incorporating the lard while kneading. § Place the tomatoes in boiling water for 1 minute, then peel. Cut them in two, remove the seeds and cut in half again. § When the rising time has elapsed (about 1½ hours), knead the dough for 1 minute on a lightly floured work surface. § Break off about a third of the dough and set aside. § Roll the rest into a disk about 12 in (30 cm) in diameter. § Oil a 9-in (23-cm) springform pan and line the base and sides with the dough. § Cover with the cheese, then the tomatoes. Sprinkle with salt and pepper. Add the anchovies, onion, and lard. § Roll the remaining dough into a disk as large as the springform pan and cover the filling. Seal the dish by folding the edges of the first sheet of dough over the second to make a border. Prick the surface with a fork and brush with the oil. Cover with a cloth and set aside to rise for about 30 minutes. § Bake in a preheated oven at 400°F/200°C/gas 6 for 30 minutes.

Torta al formaggio
Cheese flat bread

An Easter speciality from Umbria, this cheese flat bread is traditionally served piping hot with sliced ham, prosciutto, salami, mortadella and other preserved meats.

Makes: 1 flat bread, about 10 in (25 cm) in diameter; Preparation: 40 minutes; Rising time: about 4 hours; Cooking: 40 minutes; Level of difficulty: Simple

Mix the yeast with the water, add the sugar and set aside for 10 minutes. § Combine the eggs with the oil in a bowl. § Combine the flour in a bowl with the salt. Stir in the yeast mixture and the eggs until the flour absorbs all the ingredients. The dough will be soft and sticky. § Mix for 6–8 minutes with a wooden spoon. Cover with a cloth and set aside to rise for 2 hours. § When the rising time has elapsed, add the cheese and pepper and mix again for 3–4 minutes. § Oil and flour a 10-in (25-cm) springform pan. Fill with the dough, cover with a cloth and set aside to rise for 2 hours. § Bake in a preheated oven at 375°F/190°C/gas 5 for 40 minutes. § Serve hot.

Torta di bietole
Swiss chard pie

Makes: 1 filled bread, about 10 in (25 cm) in diameter; Preparation: 45 minutes + 30 minutes standing; Cooking: 25-30 minutes; Level of difficulty: Medium

Put the flour in a mixing bowl and add the salt, water, and oil. Stir well the knead as explained on page 13 until the dough is soft and elastic. Cover and set aside for 30 minutes. § For the filling, heat 3 tablespoons of oil in a sauté pan, add the onion and, after 2–3 minutes, the Swiss chard, marjoram, and borage. Sauté over medium-low heat for 5–7 minutes. § Transfer to a mixing bowl and leave to cool. § Add the egg, cheese, salt, and pepper, and mix well. § Break off about a third of the dough and set aside. § Roll the rest into a disk about 12 in (30 cm) in diameter. Use as little additional flour as possible when rolling the dough; it should be very elastic. § Oil a 10-in (25-cm) springform pan and line the base and sides with the dough. § Spread with the filling. § Roll the remaining dough into a disk as large as the springform pan and cover the filling. Seal the dish by folding the edges of the first sheet of dough over the second to make a border. § Brush the surface with the remaining oil, and bake in a preheated oven at 400°F/200°C/gas 6 for 25–30 minutes. § Serve hot.

■ INGREDIENTS

DOUGH
• 2½ cups (8 oz/250 g) unbleached white flour
• 1 teaspoon salt
• ½ cup (4 fl oz/125 ml) cold water
• 3 tablespoons extra-virgin olive oil

FILLING
• 4 tablespoons extra-virgin olive oil
• 2 tablespoons onion, finely chopped
• 1¼ lb (600 g) Swiss chard (silver beet), boiled squeezed, and chopped
• 1 tablespoon marjoram
• 4 leaves borage, chopped
• 1 egg
• ¾ cup (3 oz/90 g) Parmesan cheese, freshly grated
• salt and freshly ground black pepper

Wine: a dry white (Tocai)

Crostata al formaggio
Cheese, cream, and speck pie

Makes: 1 pie, about 9 in (23 cm) in diameter; Preparation: 10 minutes + 40 minutes for the pastry; Cooking: 30-35 minutes; Level of difficulty: Medium

Prepare the pastry base. § Combine the eggs in a bowl with salt and pepper to taste. Add the Emmental and cream. § Remove the pastry base from the refrigerator and discard the plastic wrap. Sprinkle the speck over the base, then pour the egg, cheese, and cream mixture over the top. § Bake in a preheated oven at 350°F/180°C/gas 4 for 30–35 minutes. Raise the oven temperature a little for the last 5 minutes, so that the pie crust will turn golden brown. § Serve hot.

■ INGREDIENTS

DOUGH
• 1 quantity *Ricotta pastry* (see recipe p. 16)
• 3 eggs, lightly beaten
• salt and freshly ground black pepper
• 1 cup (4 oz/125 g) Emmental cheese, freshly grated
• ⅔ cup (5 fl oz/150 ml) light (single) cream
• ¾ cup (3½ oz/100 g) speck, coarsely chopped

Right: Crostata di ricotta

■ INGREDIENTS

DOUGH
- 1 quantity *Special* or *Plain pastry* (see recipes p. 16)

TOPPING
- 1¼ cups (10 oz/300 g) fresh Ricotta cheese
- 2 eggs, beaten
- ¼ cup (2 oz/60 g) ham + ⅓ cup (3 oz/90 g) mortadella, chopped
- ½ cup (2 oz/60 g) spicy Provolone cheese, grated
- 2 tablespoons light cream
- salt and pepper

CROSTATA DI RICOTTA
Ricotta pie

Makes: 1 pie, about 9 in (23 cm) in diameter; Preparation: 30 minutes + 40 minutes for the pastry; Cooking: 40 minutes; Level of difficulty: Medium

Prepare the pastry base. § Combine the Ricotta, eggs, ham, mortadella, Provolone, cream, salt, and pepper in a mixing bowl. § Remove the pastry base from the refrigerator and discard the plastic wrap. § Spread the base evenly with the filling and bake in a preheated oven at 375°F/190°C/gas 5 for about 40 minutes, or until the top is golden brown. § Leave to cool and serve at room temperature. This pie can be prepared ahead of time.

Pizza di scarola

Filled bread with Belgian endive or escarole

This is a traditional recipe for a Christmas Eve dish from Campania, the region around Naples, in the south. Use either endives or escarole, whichever is easier to find.

Makes: 1 filled bread, 9 in (23 cm) in diameter; Preparation: 45 minutes; Rising time: about 2 hours; Cooking: 30 minutes; Level of difficulty: Medium

Prepare the dough as shown on pages 12–13. § Blanch the Belgian endive or escarole in 5 pints (2 liters) of boiling water for 2–3 minutes. Drain, squeeze out excess moisture, and coarsely chop. § Sauté the garlic in two-thirds of the oil until it turns light gold. Discard the garlic. § Add the endive (or escarole), capers, and olives and sauté over medium heat for 7–8 minutes. § Turn off the heat and add the anchovies. Stir well and set aside to cool. § When the rising time has elapsed (about 1½ hours), knead the dough for half a minute on a lightly floured work surface. § Break off about a third of the dough and set aside. § Roll the rest into a disk about 12 in (30 cm) in diameter. § Grease a 9-in (23-cm) springform pan with the lard and line the base and sides with the dough. § Taste the filling and season with salt if necessary. Spread the base with the filling and, if liked, sprinkle with the raisins. § Roll the remaining dough into a disk as large as the springform pan and cover the filling. Seal the dish by folding the edges of the first sheet of dough over the second to make a border. Brush the surface with the remaining oil, cover, and set aside to rise for 30 minutes. § Bake in a preheated oven at 400°F/200°C/gas 6 for 30 minutes. § This dish is usually served hot, but it is also delicious at room temperature.

INGREDIENTS

DOUGH
- ½ oz (15 g) fresh yeast or package active dry yeast
- 1 teaspoon sugar
- about ¾ cup (200 ml/ 7 fl oz) lukewarm water
- 3 cups (12 oz/350 g) unbleached white flour
- 2 teaspoons salt

FILLING
- 2½ lb (1.25 kg) Belgian endives or escarole, cleaned and washed
- 1 clove garlic, cut in half
- ½ cup (4 fl oz/125 ml) extra-virgin olive oil
- 2 tablespoons capers
- 1 cup (3½ oz/100 g) black olives, pitted
- 8 anchovy fillets, chopped
- 1 tablespoon lard
- salt
- 1 tablespoon raisins, rinsed in warm water (optional)

Wine: a dry white (Greco di Tufo)

VARIATIONS
– Add a generous grinding of fresh black pepper to the dough.
– Sprinkle the filling with pine nuts in place of, or together with, the raisins.

Right:
Pizza di scarola

Torta di asparagi
Asparagus pie

Makes: 1 pie, about 10 in (25 cm) in diameter; Preparation: 40 minutes + 30 minutes standing; Cooking: 35-40 minutes; Level of difficulty: Medium

Asparagus pie is prepared in the same way as the Onion pie on page 104. § Steam the asparagus, drain, and discard all but the green tips. Divide the tips into 2–3 strips and sauté for a few minutes in the butter. § Mix with the egg, cheese, and other ingredients and proceed as with the Onion pie. § In the same way it is possible to use French beans (about 1¾ lb/800 g), boiled and sautéed briefly in butter, or porcini mushrooms (about 1¾ lb/800 g) sautéed for 7–8 minutes over a high heat with 4 tablespoons extra-virgin olive oil, 2 cloves finely chopped garlic, and 2 tablespoons finely chopped parsley.

■ INGREDIENTS

DOUGH
- 1 quantity *Plain pastry* (see recipe p. 16)

FILLING
- 3 lb (1.5 kg) fresh asparagus
- 4 eggs
- ½ cup (2 oz/60 g) Parmesan cheese, freshly grated
- 1 cup (8 oz/250 g) soft Ricotta cheese
- 3 tablespoons butter
- 3 tablespoons oil
- salt and freshly ground black pepper

Wine: a dry white (Galestro)

Torta rustica
Filled bread with cheese, ham, and salami

Makes: 1 filled bread, about 9 in (23 cm) in diameter; Preparation: 35 minutes; Rising time: about 2 hours; Cooking: 25-30 minutes; Level of difficulty: Medium

Prepare the dough as shown on pages 12–13, setting the lard aside. § Combine all the filling ingredients, except the oil, in a bowl, and mix. § When the rising time has elapsed (about 1½ hours), knead the dough for half a minute on a lightly floured work surface. § Flatten the dough, sprinkle with the lard and knead again. § Break off about a third of the dough and set aside. § Roll the rest into a disk about 12 in (30 cm) in diameter. § Oil a 9-in (23-cm) springform pan and line the base and sides with the dough. § Spread with the filling. § Roll the remaining dough into a disk as large as the springform pan and cover the filling. Seal the dish by folding the edges of the first sheet of dough over the second to make a border. Brush the surface with the oil, cover with a cloth and set aside to rise for 30 minutes. § Bake in a preheated oven at 400°F/200°C/gas 6 for about 25–30 minutes. § Serve warm or cold.

■ INGREDIENTS

DOUGH
- ½ oz (15 g) fresh yeast or 1 package active dry yeast
- 1 teaspoon sugar
- about ¾ cup (7 fl oz/ 200 ml) lukewarm water
- 3 cups (12 oz/350 g) unbleached white flour
- 2 teaspoons salt
- ⅓ cup (3 oz/90 g) lard

FILLING
- ¾ cup (7 oz/225 g) Ricotta cheese
- 1¾ cups (7 oz/225 g) Pecorino cheese, grated
- ⅔ cup (2½ oz/75 g) prosciutto, diced
- ½ cup (2 oz/60 g) salami, diced
- 1 egg
- salt and pepper
- 2 tablespoons extra-virgin olive oil

Right: Torta di asparagi

■ INGREDIENTS

DOUGH

- ½ oz (15 g) fresh yeast or 1 package active dry yeast
- 2 teaspoons sugar
- 3–4 tablespoons lukewarm milk (or water)
- 2½ cups (8 oz/250 g) unbleached white flour
- 1 heaped teaspoon salt
- ⅔ cup (5 oz/150 g) butter, at room temperature, in thin slices
- 4 eggs, lightly beaten

FILLING

- 14 oz (450 g) ripe tomatoes
- 2 tablespoons extra-virgin olive oil
- 10 oz (300 g) Mozzarella cheese, sliced
- salt and freshly ground black pepper
- 8–10 leaves fresh basil, torn
- 5 oz (150 g) prosciutto, sliced and cut in strips
- 4 tablespoons Parmesan cheese, freshly grated
- 1 egg, beaten
- 2 tablespoons butter

Wine: a dry white (Pinot Grigio)

PIZZA ALLA CAMPOFRANCO
Neapolitan filled bread

Makes: 1 filled bread, about 9 in (23 cm) in diameter; Preparation: 45 minutes; Rising time: about 3 hours; Cooking: 25-30 minutes; Level of difficulty: Medium

Crumble the yeast into a bowl and add the sugar. Mix with the milk (or water) and set aside for 5 minutes. § Put the flour in a mixing bowl, sprinkle with salt and make a hollow in the center. Fill with the yeast mixture, butter, and eggs. Mix with a wooden spoon until the flour absorbs most of the ingredients. § Transfer to a lightly floured work surface. Use a spatula to remove all the mixture from the bowl. § Knead for several minutes until the dough becomes soft and elastic. § Place in a bowl, cover with a cloth, and set aside to rise for 2 hours. § Place the tomatoes in boiling water for 1 minute, then peel, cut in half, and remove the seeds. § Sauté the tomatoes in the oil over high heat for 3–4 minutes. Shake the pan from time to time to move and turn the tomatoes, rather than stirring them. § Butter and flour a 9-in (23-cm) springform pan. § When the rising time has elapsed (about 2 hours), transfer the dough to a lightly floured work surface and tap lightly with your fingers so that it contracts a little. § Break off about a third of the dough and set aside. § Place the rest in the springform pan and spread by hand to line the base and sides of the pan. § Cover with half the Mozzarella, followed by the tomatoes. Sprinkle with salt and pepper, scatter with the basil, and cover with the prosciutto and remaining Mozzarella. Sprinkle with the Parmesan and, if liked, more pepper. § Roll the remaining dough into a disk as large as the springform pan. Brush the edges of the dough with half the beaten egg. Cover the filling with the dough and seal the edges by pressing them together lightly with your fingers. § Cover with a cloth and set aside to rise for about 1 hour. § Brush the surface of the dish with the remaining egg and bake in a preheated oven at 400°F/200°C/gas 6 for 25–30 minutes. § Serve hot.

Left: *Pizza alla Campofranco*

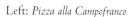

CROSTATA DI SPINACI
Spinach pie

Makes: 1 pie, about 9 in (23 cm) in diameter; Preparation: 10 minutes + time for the pastry; Cooking: 40 minutes; Level of difficulty: Medium

Prepare the pastry base. § Mix the spinach and Ricotta in a bowl. Add the Parmesan, eggs, cream, salt, pepper, and, if liked, nutmeg. Mix well. § Remove the pastry base from the refrigerator and discard the plastic wrap. § Spread evenly with the topping and sprinkle with the bread crumbs. § Sprinkle with the butter and bake in a preheated oven at 350°F/180°C/gas 4 for about 40 minutes. § This pie can be served hot or at room temperature.

■ INGREDIENTS

DOUGH
• 1 quantity *Plain pastry* (see recipe p. 16)

TOPPING
• 1½ lb (750 g) spinach, cooked, squeezed dry, and chopped
• 1 cup (8 oz/250 g) Ricotta cheese
• ½ cup (2 oz/60 g) Parmesan cheese, freshly grated
• 2 eggs, beaten
• ⅔ cup (5 fl oz/150 ml) cream
• salt and black pepper
• nutmeg
• 2 tablespoons bread crumbs
• 2 tablespoons butter, chopped

PIZZA ALLA BARESE
Filled bread with tomatoes, olives, and onion

Makes: 1 filled bread, about 9 in (23 cm) in diameter; Preparation: 40 minutes; Rising time: about 2 hours; Cooking: 30 minutes; Level of difficulty: Medium

Prepare the dough as explained on pages 12–13. § Plunge the tomatoes into boiling water for 1–2 minutes, then into cold. Peel and cut into segments, removing the seeds. § Heat 3 tablespoons of oil in a sauté pan. Add the onion and, after 1 minute, the tomatoes. Cook over high heat for 3–4 minutes, stirring as little as possible to avoid crushing the tomatoes. Remove from heat. § Add the olives to the tomato mixture. Season with salt and pepper. § When the rising time has elapsed (about 1½ hours), knead the dough on a lightly floured work surface for half a minute. § Break off a third of the dough and set aside. Roll the rest into a disk about 12 in (30 cm) in diameter. § Oil a 9-in (23-cm) springform pan and line the base and sides with the dough. § Spread with the tomato mixture and sprinkle with the Ricotta. § Roll the remaining dough into a disk as large as the springform pan and cover the filling. Seal the dish by folding the edges of the first sheet of dough over the second to make a border. Brush the surface with the oil, cover with a cloth and set aside to rise for 30 minutes. § Bake in a preheated oven at 400°F/ 200°C/gas 6 for about 30 minutes. § Serve hot.

■ INGREDIENTS

DOUGH
• ½ oz (15 g) fresh yeast or 1 package active dry yeast
• 1 teaspoon sugar
• about ¾ cup (7 fl oz/ 200 ml) lukewarm water
• 3 cups (12 oz/350 g) unbleached white flour
• 2 teaspoons salt

FILLING
• 1 lb (500 g) ripe tomatoes
• ⅓ cup (3½ fl oz/100 ml) extra-virgin olive oil
• 1 medium onion, sliced
• ¾ cup (3 oz/90 g) black olives, pitted (stoned), and cut in 4 lengthwise
• salt and freshly ground black pepper
• 2 cups (8 oz/250 g) Ricotta salata cheese, flaked

Wine: a dry red (Bardolino)

Right: *Crostata di spinaci*

Torta pasqualina
Easter pie

This extraordinary dish comes from Liguria, the region around the city of Genoa. It is not quick or easy to make but, if you persevere, it is well worth the effort. According to tradition, the pie should be made with 33 sheets of pastry – Christ's age when he died. Nowadays, the number is usually reduced, as in the following version.

Makes: 1 pie, about 10 in (25 cm) in diameter; Preparation: 1½ hours + 40 minutes standing; Cooking: 50 minutes; Level of difficulty: Complicated

Put the flour in a mixing bowl, sprinkle with salt, and make a hollow in the center. Fill with the oil and water. Mix with a wooden spoon until most of the flour has been absorbed. § Transfer the mixture to a lightly floured work surface and knead until the dough is smooth and elastic. § Divide into 15 portions, 14 the same size and one slightly larger. Cover with a damp cloth and set aside for 30 minutes. § Remove the white part from the stalks of the Swiss chard, rinse well, and cook for 5–7 minutes in a little salted, boiling water. Drain, squeeze, and coarsely chop. § Sauté the onion, garlic, and parsley in 3 tablespoons of oil for 2 minutes over medium-low heat. § Add the Swiss chard and cook, stirring frequently, for about 5 minutes. Turn off the heat, add the marjoram, stir well and set aside to cool. § Combine the Ricotta, cream, flour, and 2 eggs in a bowl, season with salt and pepper, and mix well. § Roll out the larger piece of dough to obtain a very thin disk large enough to cover the base of the springform pan. § Oil the springform pan and line with the dough. Stretch the dough carefully so that it covers the sides and overlaps a little. The dough should be very thin, almost transparent. Brush with oil. § Prepare another 6 sheets of dough, large enough to cover the base and three-quarters of the sides of the springform pan. Place them in the pan one by one, brushing their surfaces with oil, except for the last one. § Spread the Swiss chard evenly over the top sheet and sprinkle with half the Parmesan. Drizzle with 2 tablespoons of the oil and cover with the Ricotta mixture. § Use the back of a spoon to make 6 fairly deep hollows evenly spaced in the filling. Place a little butter in each hollow, then break an egg into each, taking care to keep the yolks intact. Season with salt and pepper, drizzle each egg with a few drops of olive oil, and sprinkle with the remaining Parmesan. §

■ INGREDIENTS

DOUGH
- 4 cups (1 lb/500 g) unbleached white flour
- 2 teaspoons salt
- 2 tablespoons extra-virgin olive oil
- 1 cup (8 fl oz/250 ml) water

FILLING
- 2 lb (1 kg) fresh Swiss chard (silver beet)
- 2 heaped tablespoons onion, finely chopped
- 1 clove garlic, finely chopped (optional)
- 1 tablespoon parsley, finely chopped
- ⅓ cup (3½ fl oz/100 ml) extra-virgin olive oil
- 1 heaped teaspoon fresh marjoram
- ¾ cup (7 oz/200 g) soft Ricotta cheese
- ⅓ cup (3½ fl oz/100 ml) fresh cream
- 1 tablespoon all-purpose (plain) flour
- 8 eggs
- salt and freshly ground black pepper
- ½ cup (2 oz/60 g) Parmesan cheese, freshly grated
- 2 tablespoons butter

Wine: a dry white (Colli di Luni)

Right: *Torta pasqualina*

Use the remaining dough to make another 6 sheets about the same size as the springform pan. Place them over the filling one by one, brushing their surfaces with oil. § Fold back the edges of the first sheet, sealing the edges of the sheets inside, and forming a border around the pie. Brush the surface with oil and prick with a fork, taking care not to break the egg yolks inside. § Bake in a preheated oven at 375°F/190°C/gas 5 for 50 minutes. § Serve lukewarm or at room temperature.

VARIATION
– Replace the Swiss chard with 8 globe artichokes, previously cleaned, sliced, and cooked with the onion, garlic, and parsley as above, but using 2½ tablespoons of butter instead of the oil.

INGREDIENTS

DOUGH

- 3 cups (12 oz/350 g) unbleached white flour
- 1 teaspoon salt
- ⅓ cup (3½ oz/90 g) lard (or butter), thinly sliced and at room temperature
- about ⅔ cup (5 fl oz/ 150 ml) cold water

FILLING

- 2½ tablespoons lard (or butter)
- 1 cup (4 oz/125 g) pancetta, chopped
- 1 tablespoon onion, chopped
- 1 clove garlic, finely chopped
- 1 tablespoon parsley, finely chopped
- 1 lb (500 g) spinach
- 1¼ cup (4 oz/125 g) Parmesan cheese, freshly grated
- 2 eggs
- salt and freshly ground black pepper
- dash of nutmeg (optional)
- 1 tablespoon light (single) cream (or milk)

Wine: a dry red (Sangiovese di Romagna)

SCARPAZZONE

Filled bread with spinach, pancetta, and Parmesan cheese

This traditional bread comes from the Emilia-Romagna region, in central Italy.

Makes: 1 pie, about 9 in (23 cm) in diameter; Preparation: 40 minutes + 30 minutes standing; Cooking: 30 minutes; Level of difficulty: Medium

Combine the flour in a bowl with the salt. Make a hollow in the flour and fill with the lard and water. Mix with a fork until the ingredients are roughly amalgamated. § Transfer to a lightly floured work surface and knead until the dough is smooth and soft. Cover with a cloth and set aside for at least 30 minutes. § Clean the spinach, rinse well, and cook for 5–7 minutes in a little salted, boiling water. Drain, squeeze, and coarsely chop. § Place 2 tablespoons of lard in a large sauté pan with the pancetta, onion, garlic, and parsley. Sauté over medium-low heat for a few minutes. Add the spinach and cook, stirring frequently, for 8–10 minutes. § Transfer the mixture to a bowl and set aside to cool. § Add the Parmesan, eggs, salt, and pepper, and, if liked, a little nutmeg. § Break off about a third of the dough and set aside. § Roll the rest into a disk about 11 in (28 cm) in diameter. § Grease a springform pan with the remaining lard and line the base and sides with the dough. § Spread evenly with the filling. § Roll the remaining dough into a disk slightly larger than the springform pan and cover the filling. Seal the dish by folding the edges of the first sheet of dough over the second to make a border. Prick the surface with a fork and brush with the cream. § Bake in a preheated oven at 375°F/190°C/gas 5 for about 30 minutes. § Serve hot or at room temperature.

Left: Scarpazzone

VARIATION
– Replace the spinach with the same quantity of Swiss chard (silver beet), or use equal quantities of each.

CROSTATA DI CIPOLLE
Onion pie

Makes: 1 pie, about 9 in (23 cm) in diameter; Preparation: 40 minutes + 40 minutes for the pastry; Cooking: 40 minutes; Level of difficulty: Medium

Prepare the pastry. § Sauté the onions in the butter over low heat for 25–30 minutes, stirring frequently. When cooked, the onions should be soft and golden brown. § Lightly beat the egg in a bowl, then add the milk and the flour, mixing well so that no lumps form. Season with salt and pepper. § Remove the pastry base from the refrigerator and discard the plastic wrap. § Cover the base with a sheet of foil, pressing it down carefully so that it adheres to the pastry. § Bake in a preheated oven at 350°F/180°C/gas 4 for 15 minutes. § Take the pie plate or springform pan out of the oven and, using the palm of a gloved hand, carefully press the base down so that it contracts a little. § Discard the foil and return the pie to the oven for 5 minutes more. § Take the base out again, spread evenly with the onion mixture and pour the egg and milk mixture over the top. § Bake for 20 minutes more. § Serve hot.

■ INGREDIENTS

DOUGH
• 1 quantity *Plain pastry* (see recipe p. 16)

TOPPING
• 2 lb (1 kg) onions, sliced
• 3 oz (90 g) butter
• 1 egg
• ¾ cup (6 fl oz/180 ml) milk
• 1 tablespoon flour
• salt and freshly ground black pepper

Wine: a dry white (Pinot Bianco)

CROSTATA DI PISELLI
Pea pie

Makes 1 pie, about 9 in (23 cm) in diameter; Preparation: 40 minutes + 40 minutes for the pastry; Cooking: 40 minutes; Level of difficulty: Medium

Prepare the pastry base. § Parboil the peas in a pot of salted, boiling water for 5–10 minutes. Drain and place in a small, heavy-bottomed saucepan with 2 tablespoons of melted butter. Sauté over medium-low heat, stirring frequently, for about 5 minutes, or until the peas are tender. Season with salt. § Remove the pastry base from the refrigerator and discard the plastic wrap. Cover the base with a sheet of foil, pressing it down carefully so that it adheres to the pastry. § Bake in a preheated oven at 350°F/180°C/gas 4 for 15 minutes. § Take the pie plate or springform pan out of the oven and, using the palm of a gloved hand, carefully press the base down so that it contracts a little. § Discard the foil and return the base to the oven for 5 minutes

■ INGREDIENTS

DOUGH
• 1 quantity *Plain* or *Ricotta pastry* (see recipes p. 16)

TOPPING
• 1 cup (6 oz/180 g) fresh or frozen peas
• 3 tablespoons butter
• salt and freshly ground black pepper
• 1 tablespoon flour
• about ¾ cup (6 fl oz/ 180 ml) hot milk

Right:
Crostata di cipolle

- 1 egg white
- ²⁄₃ cup (3 oz/90 g) ham, coarsely chopped
- 4 tablespoons Parmesan cheese, freshly grated

Wine: a dry white (Chardonnay di Franciacorta)

more. § In the meantime, melt the remaining butter in a small saucepan. Add the flour and cook over low heat for 2 minutes, stirring constantly. Add the milk, a little at a time, stirring continuously. In about 5 minutes you will obtain a smooth béchamel; it should be rather dense, so do not use too much milk. § Beat the egg white until stiff and combine with the peas, béchamel, ham, Parmesan, salt, and pepper. § Mix well and pour into the pastry base. § Bake in a preheated oven at 350°F/180°C/gas 4 for about 30 minutes or until the surface is light gold. § Serve hot.

Crostata di zucchine
Zucchini pie

Makes: 1 pie, about 9 in (23 cm) in diameter; Preparation: 40 minutes + 40 minutes for the pastry; Cooking: 35-40 minutes; Level of difficulty: Medium

Prepare the pastry base. § Soak the mushrooms in a little warm water for about 15 minutes. Drain and coarsely chop. § Remove the rind from the pancetta and sauté over medium-high heat for 3–4 minutes. Set aside, discarding the fat that the pancetta produces. § Heat the oil in the same sauté pan and cook the zucchini and mushrooms over medium heat for 10–15 minutes, stirring frequently. Season with salt and pepper and set aside to cool. § Lightly beat the eggs in a mixing bowl, add the two cheeses, marjoram, zucchini, and pancetta. § Remove the pastry base from the refrigerator and discard the plastic wrap. § Spread the topping over the base and sprinkle with the bread crumbs. § Bake in a preheated oven at 350°F/180°C/gas 4 for 35–40 minutes. § Serve hot or warm.

■ INGREDIENTS

DOUGH
- 1 quantity *Plain pastry* (see recipe p. 16)

TOPPING
- 1 oz (30 g) dried mushrooms
- 4 oz (125 g) smoked pancetta (or bacon), sliced
- 3 tablespoons extra-virgin olive oil
- 6 medium zucchini (courgettes), sliced
- salt and freshly ground black pepper
- ¾ cup (3 oz/90 g) Pecorino cheese, flaked
- 3 tablespoons Parmesan cheese, freshly grated
- 2 eggs
- 1 tablespoon marjoram
- 1 tablespoon bread crumbs

Wine: a dry white (Pinot Grigio)

Crostata di porri
Leek pie

Makes: 1 pie, about 9 in (23 cm) in diameter; Preparation: 40 minutes; Cooking: 40 minutes + 40 minutes for the pastry; Level of difficulty: Medium

Prepare the pastry. § Clean the leeks and slice thinly, using the white part only. § Sauté the leeks in 3 tablespoons of butter over medium-low heat for 15–20 minutes. Season with salt and pepper and set aside to cool. § In the meantime, melt the remaining butter in a small saucepan. Add the flour and cook over low heat for 2 minutes, stirring constantly. Add the milk, a little at a time, stirring continuously. In 4–5 minutes you will obtain a smooth béchamel; it should be rather dense, so do not use too much milk. § Beat the egg white until stiff and combine with the leeks, béchamel, Gruyère, salt, and pepper. Mix well. § Remove the pastry base from the refrigerator and discard the plastic wrap. § Pour the leek mixture over the top and sprinkle with the Parmesan. Bake in a preheated oven at 350°F/180°C/gas 4 for 40 minutes. § Serve hot.

■ INGREDIENTS

DOUGH
- 1 quantity *Special pastry* (see recipe, p. 16)

TOPPING
- 2 lb (1 kg) leeks
- 4 tablespoons butter
- salt and black pepper
- 1 tablespoon flour
- ¾ cup (7 fl oz/200 ml) hot milk
- 1 egg white
- 4 tablespoons Gruyère (or Emmental) cheese, freshly grated
- 2 tablespoons Parmesan cheese, freshly grated

Right: Crostata di porri

FRIED DISHES

Fried tidbits and fritters
are common in Italian regional cooking.
These are some of the tastiest.

BORLENGHI
Lard fritters

This classic recipe comes from Emilia, the area around Bologna. In the richer modern version, the water is replaced by milk and an egg is added.

Makes: about 10 fritters; Preparation: 2 minutes; Cooking: 15 minutes; Level of difficulty: Simple

Mix the flour, water, and salt together in a bowl. The mixture should be fairly liquid. § Place a cast-iron or iron pan not larger than 8 in (20 cm) in diameter over high heat. Lightly grease with a thin slice of lard. § When the lard is hot, add 2 tablespoons of the mixture and tip the pan this way and that so that the mixture spreads evenly, forming a thin layer that will set almost immediately. § After 30–40 seconds turn the fritter over with the aid of a wooden spatula and cook on the other side. § Repeat the process until all the mixture is used up. § Traditionally, these fritters are served hot, lightly spread with a mixture of lard, fresh rosemary, and finely chopped garlic, sprinkled with grated Pecorino or Parmesan cheese, and folded in four.

VARIATION
– Use extra-virgin olive oil to grease the pan instead of lard.

■ INGREDIENTS

- 1¼ cups (5 oz/150 g) unbleached white flour
- 1¼ cups (10 fl oz/300 ml) water
- 1 teaspoon salt
- 1 tablespoon lard

Wine: a dry red (Gutturnio)

CRESCENTE
Emilian fritters

Emilian regional cookery has many fried dishes. They are usually served with a mixed platter of ham, prosciutto, mortadella, and other deli meats, and cheeses.

Serves: 4; Preparation: 30 minutes + 30 minutes standing; Cooking: 15 minutes; Level of difficulty: Medium

Put the flour in a bowl with the salt, and mix. Make a hollow in the center and fill with the olive oil and milk. § Mix well and transfer to a lightly floured work surface. Knead until the dough is soft and smooth. § Cover with a cloth and set aside for 30 minutes. § Roll the dough out to about ½ in (1 cm) thickness. Cut in strips four fingers wide and roll each strip to about ⅛ in (3 mm) thick. § Cut the strips into diamond-shapes with sides 3 in (7.5 cm) long and place on clean paper towels. § Fry the fritters 3 or 4 at a time in 1¼ in (3 cm) of very hot oil. They will swell and often turn over by themselves. Cook for about 1 minute, or until they are golden brown. § Drain well and place on paper towels to absorb excess oil. § Serve hot.

■ INGREDIENTS

- 3¼ cups (13 oz/380 g) unbleached white flour
- 1 teaspoon salt
- ½ cup (4 fl oz/125 ml) extra-virgin olive oil
- about ⅔ cup (5 fl oz/ 150 ml) warm milk
- 2 cups oil, for frying

Wine: a dry red (Colli Piacentini Barbera)

Right:
Crescente

Torta fritta
Fried gnocchi

Also known as gnocco fritto, *this recipe also comes from Emilia, in central Italy.*

Serves: 4; Preparation: 30 minutes; Rising time: about 1½ hours; Cooking: 15-20 minutes; Level of difficulty: Medium

Prepare the yeast as explained on page 12. § Put the flour in a bowl and sprinkle with salt. Make a hollow in the center and fill with the lard (or butter). § Pour in the yeast mixture and the remaining water and mix the ingredients with a fork. § Transfer the dough to a lightly floured work surface. Knead until the dough is soft and smooth. § Shape the dough into a ball, cover with a cloth and set aside to rise for 1½ hours, or until it doubles in volume. § When the rising time has elapsed, roll the dough out to a thickness of about ½ in (1 cm). § Cut into diamond-shapes with sides 2 in (4–5 cm) long and place on clean paper towels. § Fry a few shapes at a time in about 1½ in (3 cm) of very hot oil. § Drain when golden brown on both sides and drain on paper towels. § Sprinkle with salt and serve hot.

Ciacci
Chestnut flour fritters

This is another delicious recipe from Emilia. Something very similar, called necci, *though cooked in a waffle-iron, is made near Pistoia, in Tuscany. Both are served with soft, fresh cheeses, such as Ricotta.*

Serves: 4; Preparation: 3-4 minutes; Cooking: 15-20 minutes; Level of difficulty: Simple

Mix the flour with the water and salt using a food processor or hand blender to prevent lumps from forming. The mixture should be fairly liquid. § Grease the bottom of a cast-iron or iron pan no larger than 8 in (20 cm) in diameter with a little olive oil. Place over high heat. § When the oil is very hot, add 2–3 tablespoons of the mixture to cover the bottom of the pan in a thin layer. Turn over after about 1 minute, or when the mixture is well set, and cook on the other side. § Repeat the process until all the mixture is used up. Stack the fritters on a plate resting on a pot of boiling water to keep them warm. § Serve immediately.

Left: Ciacci

PANZEROTTI
Filled fritters

I have suggested two simple fillings. Mix the ingredients in a bowl until smooth and fill the panzerotti *as directed.*

Serves: 4; Preparation: 25-30 minutes; Rising time: 1 hour; Cooking: 15 minutes; Level of difficulty: Simple

Prepare the dough as explained on pages 12–13. § When the rising time has elapsed (about 1 hour), transfer the dough to a lightly floured work surface and knead for 1 minute. § Shape into a long thin loaf and divide into 10–12 portions. § Flatten the dough with your hands into small disks about 3 in (8 cm) in diameter. § Place a heaped teaspoon of filling on one half of each and spread a little. Fold the dough over the top to form crescent shapes. Moisten the edges with 2–3 drops of water and seal by pressing down with your fingertips. § Fry the panzerotti 5 or 6 at a time in about 1¼ in (3 cm) of very hot oil. § When browned, drain well, and transfer to paper towels to absorb excess oil. § Serve hot.

■ INGREDIENTS

- ½ oz (15 g) fresh yeast or 1 package active dry yeast
- 1 teaspoon sugar
- ⅔ cup (5 fl oz/150 ml) lukewarm water
- 3 cups (12 oz/350 g) unbleached white flour
- 1–2 teaspoons salt
- oil for frying

FILLINGS:
- **Mixed cheese:** 3 oz (90 g) Ricotta cheese; 2 oz (60 g) Provolone cheese, freshly grated; 2 oz (60 g) Mozzarella cheese, diced; 2 oz (60 g) smoked Provola cheese, diced; 1 tablespoon milk, 1 teaspoon parsley, finely chopped
- **Ham and Ricotta:** 1 cup (5 oz/150 g) ham, coarsely chopped; 1 cup (8 oz/250 g) Ricotta cheese; black pepper

CHIZZE
Parmesan fritters

Serves: 4; Preparation: 30 minutes; Cooking: 15-20 minutes; Level of difficulty: Medium

Put the flour in a bowl, add the salt, lard, and butter and mix well with a fork. Add the water gradually, and when nearly all the flour has been absorbed, transfer the mixture to a lightly floured work surface. § Knead until the dough is smooth and elastic. § Roll out to about ⅛ in (3 mm) thick and cut into 3-in (8-cm) squares. Place a slice of Parmesan on one half of each square and fold the dough over the top to form a triangle. Moisten the edges with 2–3 drops of water and seal by pressing down with your fingertips. § Fry the fritters 3 or 4 at a time in about 1¼ in (3 cm) of very hot oil. § When browned, drain well and transfer to paper towels to absorb excess oil. § Serve hot or at room temperature.

VARIATIONS
– Replace the Parmesan with Emmental or Fontina cheese.
– Omit the Parmesan and fill the fritters with a mixture of coarsely chopped prosciutto and lightly boiled and chopped Swiss chard (silver beet), sautéed in butter or olive oil with half an anchovy fillet.

■ INGREDIENTS

- 2¾ cups (10 oz/300 g) unbleached white flour
- 1 teaspoon salt
- 2 tablespoons lard
- 2 tablespoons butter
- about ½ cup (4 fl oz/125 ml) lukewarm water
- 5 oz (150 g) Parmesan cheese, thinly sliced
- oil for frying

Wine: a dry red (Gutturnio)

Right: *Chizze*

■ INGREDIENTS

• 2¾ cups (10 oz/300 g)
  garbanzo bean
  (chickpea) flour
• 2 quarts (2 pints/1 liter)
  water
• 1 teaspoon salt
• 1 tablespoon parsley,
  finely chopped
• 2 cups oil, for frying

Wine: a dry white
(Greco di Tufo)

PANELLE
Garbanzo bean fritters

Serves: 4; Preparation: 10 minutes; Cooking: 40 minutes; Level of difficulty: Simple
Mix the flour, water and salt using a food processor or hand blender. The mixture will be fairly thick. § Transfer to a heavy-bottomed saucepan and cook over low heat for 30 minutes, stirring constantly. § Add the parsley. § Transfer the dough to a lightly oiled work surface and spread with a spatula until it is about ¼ in (½ cm) thick. § Leave to cool, then cut into diamond shapes or squares. Fry 2–3 at a time in very hot oil. § When browned, drain well, and place on paper towels. § Serve hot.

Panzerotti con pomodoro e mozzarella
Fritters filled with tomato and Mozzarella cheese

Serves: 4; Preparation: 25-30 minutes; Rising time: about 1 hour; Cooking: 25 minutes; Level of difficulty: Simple

Prepare the dough and set aside to rise. § Place the tomatoes in a small saucepan over medium heat with no added seasoning. Cook for 8–10 minutes until they reduce a little. § When the rising time has elapsed, shape the dough into panzerotti as explained on page 114. § Place a teaspoonful of tomato filling on each, cover with a slice of Mozzarella and sprinkle with salt and pepper. Moisten the edges with 2–3 drops of water and seal by pressing down with your fingertips. § Fry the panzerotti 5 or 6 at a time in about 1¼ in (3 cm) of very hot oil. § When brown, drain well, and place on paper towels to absorb excess oil. § Serve hot.

■ INGREDIENTS

DOUGH
- 1 quantity panzerotti dough (see recipe p. 114)
- 2 cups oil, for frying

FILLING
- 1¼ cups (10 oz/300 g) diced tomatoes
- 10 oz (300 g) Mozzarella cheese, sliced
- salt and freshly ground black pepper

Wine: a dry red (Chianti Classico)

Crispeddi
Anchovy fritters

Serves: 4; Preparation: 30 minutes; Rising time: 1½ hours; Cooking: 10 minutes; Level of difficulty: Simple

Prepare the yeast as explained on page 12. § Combine the flour in a bowl with the salt. Make a hollow in the flour and fill with the lard, yeast mixture and remaining water. Proceed as shown on pages 12–13. § Wash the anchovies thoroughly under cold running water and pat dry with paper towels. § When the rising time has elapsed (about 1 hour), place the dough on a lightly floured work surface and knead for 1 minute. Divide into egg-sized portions and shape into long rolls. § Cut them open lengthwise and place an anchovy fillet and a sprinkling of oregano in each. Close up the dough and place the rolls on a clean cloth. § Cover with another cloth and leave to rise for 30 minutes. § Fry the rolls 2 or 3 at a time in about 1¼ in (3 cm) of very hot oil. When browned, drain well, and place on paper towels to absorb excess oil. § Serve hot.

■ INGREDIENTS

- ½ oz (15 g) fresh yeast or 1 package active dry yeast
- ½ cup (4 fl oz/125 ml) lukewarm water
- 2¾ cups (10 oz/300 g) unbleached white flour
- 1 tablespoon lard, chopped
- 5 oz (150 g) salted anchovy fillets
- oregano
- 1 teaspoon salt
- 2 cups oil, for frying

Wine: a dry white (Corvo)

Right: *Panzerotti con pomodoro e mozzarella*

PIZZELLE
Neapolitan fritters in tomato sauce

These wonderful fritters are from Naples. The only drawback is that you can never make enough of them!

Serves: 4; Preparation: 30 minutes; Rising time: 2 hours; Cooking: 20 minutes; Level of difficulty: Simple

Prepare the yeast as explained on page 12. § Combine the flour in a large bowl with the salt, yeast mixture, and remaining water, and proceed as shown in the sequence on pages 12–13. § When the rising time has elapsed (about 1 hour), knead the dough on a floured work surface for 2–3 minutes. Divide in 8–10 portions. Shape into balls, cover with a cloth and set aside to rise for about 1 hour. § Put the tomatoes in a small saucepan, add the garlic, oregano, and oil, and cook over low heat for 15 minutes, or until they reduce. § When the second rising time has elapsed, use your hands to flatten the dough into round shapes 3 in (8 cm) in diameter. § Fry the rolls 2–3 at a time in 1¼ in (3 cm) of very hot oil. Turn the fritters halfway through cooking. They will be ready in about 1½ minutes. The fritters should be light golden brown. § Drain well and place on paper towels to absorb excess oil. § Arrange the fritters on a heated serving dish and cover each one with a tablespoon of the hot tomato sauce. § Serve hot.

■ INGREDIENTS

- ½ oz (15 g) fresh yeast or 1 package active dry yeast
- ⅔ cup (5 fl oz/150 ml) lukewarm water
- 3 cups (12 oz/350 g) unbleached white flour
- 12 oz (350 g) tomatoes, peeled and chopped
- 1 clove garlic, finely chopped
- 1 teaspoon oregano
- 1 tablespoon extra-virgin olive oil
- 1 teaspoon salt
- 2 cups oil, for frying

Wine: a dry red (Vesuvio)

MOZZARELLA IN CARROZZA
Fried Mozzarella sandwiches

Serves: 4; Preparation: 15 minutes; Cooking: 8-10 minutes; Level of difficulty: Simple

Cover four slices of bread with the Mozzarella, making sure the cheese doesn't overlap the edges of the bread. Season with salt and pepper and cover with the remaining slices of bread. Transfer to a plate and cut the sandwiches in half diagonally. § Beat the eggs and milk with salt to taste. Pour over the sandwiches and leave to stand for 2 minutes. Turn the sandwiches over so that they absorb all the egg mixture. § If liked, roll in the bread crumbs. Make sure that the edges are well soaked with the egg mixture so that they will set on contact with the hot oil, sealing the Mozzarella inside. § Fry the sandwiches 4 at a time in about 1¼ in (3 cm) of very hot oil. Turn after about 1 minute. § When browned on both sides, drain well and place on paper towels to absorb excess oil. § Serve hot.

■ INGREDIENTS

- 8 slices day-old sandwich bread, with crusts removed
- 8 oz (250 g) Mozzarella cheese, sliced
- 2 eggs
- 3 tablespoons milk
- 10 tablespoons bread crumbs (optional)
- salt and freshly ground black pepper
- 2 cups oil, for frying

Wine: a dry red (Ischia)

Right: Mozzarella in carrozza

Index